# BICYCLIST'S GUIDE TO ARIZONA

## THE BEST RIDES & TOURS IN ARIZONA

### Peter L. Bower

# A Self-Fulfillment Book

ISBN: 0-914778-36-6

For

JENNIFER

More Than a Cycling Companion

Illustrations: Leonard Wos

Published by Phoenix Books/Publishers, P. O. Box 32008, Phoenix, Arizona 85064, U.S.A.   Copyright (c) 1980 by Peter L. Bower.   All rights reserved. Manufactured in the United States of America.

ISBN:  0-914778-36-6

## ABOUT THE AUTHOR

Peter L. Bower has been an active bicylist in Arizona since the early 1970s. He has ridden throughout the state--averaging over 10,000 miles a year for several years--and has written about his experiences for such publications as Arizona, Bicycling, Young Athlete and Bike World. In 1975 Peter took his first long bicycle tour, from Phoenix, Arizona to Portland, Maine --over 3,000 miles. In 1976 Peter was selected as a Bikecentennial Tour Leader, and subsequently led three tour groups on routes in the Western United States. His longest tour was from Pueblo, Colorado to Seattle,  Washington in the summer of 1978. In addition to bicycle touring, Peter has also been active in bicycle racing. In 1978 he won the best all-around Veteran's Award. Off his bike, Peter is an English teacher at a Phoenix high school, an avid gardener and an accomplished photographer.

# CONTENTS

# Bicycling in Arizona

Whether it be pedaling in the soft evening light through suburban streets, winging down a hill on the way to *Tortilla Flat,* or puffing in slow cadence up *Mt. Lemmon,* riding a bicycle in Arizona is an extraordinary experience.

No matter the season, one or another of Arizona's climate zones offers the ten-speed enthusiast many fascinating rides. In winter, when most of the nation is snowbound, a cyclist can explore the desert area surrounding Tucson and Phoenix. In summer, when daytime in the desert is like being inside an oven, the bicyclist can escape to the high pine-covered country of Arizona's Plateaus and Highlands.

Bicycling offers an alternative method of transportation as well as a way to experience Arizona's vistas by being a part of the scenery. *Mingus Mountain, Oak Creek Canyon* and the town of *Bisbee* can really be appreciated from the saddle of a lightweight touring bicycle. To reach the top of Mingus Mountain after a slow, hot climb is like reaching the top of a personal challenge. To move rapidly down Oak Creek Canyon, feeling the crispness in the air and hearing the creek babble and birds sing, is an experience never to be forgotten. Climbing *Mule Pass* to 19th century Bisbee, one can almost hear the cries of the mules, the groaning of wooden wheels and the curses of tired miners.

*Places like Clint's Wells, Nowhere, Sunflower and Skull Valley are only dots on a map to those in a hurry to reach a destination. But on a bicycle a destination is only an excuse to experience the effort and thrill of the journey.*

And Arizona offers a myriad of fascinating routes for the person willing to take the time to search them out. The *Salt River Canyon* is only an inconvenience to those in a hurry, but to a cyclist the work of pedaling down and out of this spectacular desert canyon is what makes it memorable.

The different rides and tours described in this book were chosen because each offers something unique. Actually, any ride can be a fascinating experience. Even pedaling through suburban streets one can't help but notice the different ways individual home-owners have chosen to decorate their property.

On a bicycle one has time to appreciate a neighbor's carefully cultivated rubber tree, or marvel at another's faithful relocation of a section of desert to his front yard. One has time to stop and ask a stranger why he has chosen to display a railroad switching signal in his side yard, or what he's growing in a greenhouse half-hidden by a weeping willow. Exploring Arizona begins right at one's front door.

Once the basics of bicycling have been mastered, the desire to ride out into the scenery grows. The rides recommended in this book have been selected for the novice as well as the experienced cyclist. Many of the rides will help improve bicycling techniques.

The rides and tours vary greatly in length from a few miles to over one hundred miles. Some require a few hours of pedaling to complete, while others are day-long, overnight or even longer two-wheeled adventures.

## HOW TO USE THIS BOOK

This guide to bicycling in Arizona is designed to serve as a reference book. Information about each trip is presented from the bicyclist's point of view --why the route was chosen, what the highlights are, what difficulties may be encountered, which season is best, and a little about the history and romance of the region.

Trips were selected because they offer "good cycling"--that is light traffic, a focal point of interest, scenic beauty and adequate overnight accomodations if applicable. Trips were not disqualified because they are difficult. Routes away from the suburbs predominate.

Many of the rides follow a circular route. Like most hikers, bicyclist's prefer not to pass the same way twice if it can be avoided. Altogether, about half of the rides are loops.

For traveling on the roads in Arizona it is important that you have a road map. The best one available is the official *Arizona Road Map,* published each year by Arizona Highways, 2039 W. Lewis Ave., Phoenix, Arizona 85004. It is free.

Before setting forth on a trip of any length, mastery of shifting techniques, the ability to do minor repairs, a knowledge of how to ride safely, and a certain level of physical fitness are desirable if not mandatory. All of the recommended routes will help in the development of good riding techniques, but many of the longer rides are better enjoyed if you have mastered basic bicycling skills and are in good physical condition.

Certain of the longer rides may be broken down into shorter sections that will provide several interesting rides rather than one long one. For example, a 93-mile journey from Prescott to Flagstaff can be completed in one long day. It can also be enjoyed as a two-day tour, particularly if you want to explore Jerome and experience *Slide Rock* in Oak Creek Canyon.

Examine the longer and more difficult rides carefully before setting out.

## RIDING EFFECTIVELY

### HOW TO RIDE

In the beginning short neighborhood rides are a good way to become familar with the intricacies of a ten-speed. Regular short rides will help condition your body for longer weekend rides.practice using the different gears on level ground before attempting to climb a hill or pedaling over rolling terrain.

For both neighborhood and extended level riding, practice pedaling in a low-to-medium gear (on the front the chain should be on the smaller chain ring; on the back the chain should be in about the middle gear). Try shifting into a slightly easier-to-pedal gear just prior to coming to a stop. This will enable quicker starts and make it easier on the knees--the easiest part of the body to injure through unsound cycling practices.

Low and medium gears pedaled at a quick tempo are more effective and often make for a higher rate of speed than a slow pushing of large gears.

The gears of a ten-speed are designed to help the rider cross any kind of terrain. The number of teeth on each gear determines the size of the gear. Front chain rings usually have 52 teeth on the outer ring and 42 on the inner. A common distribution on the rear is 14-16-18-21-24. A high gear (52-14) makes the bicycle go faster, but will quickly tire the rider. Big gears are suitable for descending hills or pedaling with a strong tail wind. Low gears (41-21 or 42-24) are for climbing. On level terrain, middle-range gears are used to maintain a steady pace which will not tire the bicyclist.

As the terrain changes so should a rider change gears. The mark of an accomplished cyclist is a smooth shift with little loss of forward speed as the terrain rises and falls. Cycling effectively comes with practice. To completely master ten-speed traveling is a long-term task.

### WHO TO RIDE WITH

Riding with experienced cyclists is a good way to learn how to shift and pedal efficiently--and to meet men and women who take pleasure in transporting themselves through their own efforts. Arizona has a large number of accomplished cyclists. Phoenix, Tucson and Flagstaff have clubs that promote bicycling (see a listing at the end of this section).

Both experienced cyclists and clubs are usually eager to help newcomers gain the skills necessary to make cycling enjoyable. Throughout Arizona, groups of cyclists ride regularly on weekends. By contacting members through the organizations listed under Arizona Clubs you can obtain copies of ride schedules and learn of planned weekend tours.

Cycling is an individual activity that men and women from different backgounds may pursue collectively. Just as there are different levels of riding ability within the cycling community, there are also different reasons for riding. Some like the comradeship found on weekend breakfast rides; others the spectacular scenery encountered on tours to different parts of the state. There is also the thrill of competing against other highly conditioned athletes.

Cycling is a world within itself. With practice an individual can obtain a level of proficiency equal to his or her interests. Other cyclists with similar abilities can always be found to make the pedaling that much more enjoyable.

## HOW TO RIDE SAFELY

Bicycles are subject to the same traffic regulations as other forms of transportation that utilize the public roads. Bicyclists should obey all traffic laws. At the same time, because of their slower rate of speed when compared with cars, it is very important that they use an extra measure of caution.

Bicyclists should ride on the extreme right, with the flow of traffic, but out of the mainstream. If possible, roads other than major city arteries and high-speed highways should be utilized. In addition, peak automobile rush hours should be avoided.

A careful perusal of a city map will often lead to the discovery of alternate routes, which not only will

prove safer but often will be more scenic. On the open
highway, where alternate routes are not always possible, a good cyclist stays as far right as possible and
is constantly alert for any situation that might prove
dangerous. Whether riding in the city or country, the
cautious bicyclist dresses to be highly visible, and
gives clear hand signals before changing lanes or
turning corners. *When practical, looking motorists in
the eye before making a move is a good way to make
sure the driver knows your intentions.*

Certain equipment promotes safe cycling. A rearview
mirror helps to spot potentially dangerous situations
developing behind a rider, making it possible for the
cyclist to take evasive action if necessary. In addition to providing protection in case of a fall or col-
lision, a helmet serves to identify the wearer as one
who regularly shares the roadway with cars and trucks.
Many cyclists have reported that drivers treat helmet-
ed bikers with more respect.

It is legal for bicyclists to ride two abreast.
But there are times when it is dangerous to do so. It
is better to ride single file and be safe than be le-
gally right and endanger yourself.

*Accidents that occur while descending hills at high
rates of speed are among the most serious to cyclists.*
Learning to descend properly and how to stop when necessary or desirable makes a trip safer and provides
peace of mind when traveling down steep mountain roads
one encounters so often in Arizona.

When descending a steep grade, sit well back on the
seat and place the hands on the bottommost curve of
the handlebars in a position that will allow your fin-
gers to reach the brake levers if needed. Keep your
center of gravity low throughout the descent in order
to better balance the bicycle. Be prepared to stop
suddenly.

On turns to the right, the right knee should be
raised so that the right pedal is as far from the
ground as possible. This will minimize the chance of
the pedal striking the ground when the bike is leaning
over. On turns to the left, raise the left pedal.

It is well to remember that a loaded touring bike

descends a downgrade at a higher rate of speed due to the increased weight. If it is necessary to panic-stop, then both brake levers should be grasped and pressure applied to both wheels equally (actually it is necessary to apply more pressure to the rear brake lever because the long cable reduces stopping power).

*The most common of all bicycle mishaps, however, is not caused by downgrades or motor vehicles but by other bicycles! Sometimes they occur because one rider, staying close to another cyclist to reduce wind resistance, lets his attention wander and collides with the other cyclist. Other bike-on-bike accidents happen on bicycle paths because their narrowness forces cyclists to pass too close to each other. In addition, bicycle paths are popular with people just-learning how to ride, and with children on motocross bicycles.*

At first, bicycle riding, whether in traffic or on a bike path or descending a steep hill, will seem strange and dangerous--and it can be dangerous if you do not learn and follow safe riding practices. Learning to master such a complex and highly maneuverable machine as a bicycle is not an easy task, and requires frequent practice and vigilant attention.

## WATCHING THE WEATHER

Except for those who fly or sail boats, no other group of sports activists pays more attention to the wind and weather than do bicyclists. A check on the wind, its direction and velocity, before a ride may help determine when to leave and in what direction to proceed--or not to go at all.

Normally the wind is less of a factor on early morning rides. For this reason, and because traffic is often less, many bicyclists prefer an early start even if it means arriving at the starting place before sun-up when it is more likely to be cold during the early stages of the ride.

During the majority of the year, the wind blows from west to east across Arizona. Rides can be planned to take advantage of the west wind. A tailwind when one is tired and only interested in finishing is more than welcome.

The temperature extremes liable to be encountered on any ride are also a factor to be considered. In mid-summer desert riding is foolhardy except for a period early in the day. Evenings are usually uncomfortable because concrete and asphalt remain hot long after the sun has set. But the desert can be crossed by starting at first light and reaching adequate rest facilities before the temperatures soar.

The availability of water must also be considered in any route selection in Arizona. Not only should enough be carried to complete the ride, but it is advisable to have a sufficient amount in reserve in case of a flat tire or some other delay.

Sun screens and long-sleeved white shirts are useful on long tours. The position a bicyclist holds while pedaling, with head bent forward, causes the back of the neck--where the nerves, veins and arteries are close to the surface--to be exposed to the direct rays of the sun. A bandana, periodically dipped in water, will protect this vital area.

In winter a cyclist must consider the opposite extrene--cold. It is difficult to dress adequately for cold weather. Physical exercise keeps the body warm without unusually heavy clothing, but your extremities can freeze due to less effective blood circulation.

Not only are your hands and feet more sensitive to cold, they also come into direct contact with metal handlebars and pedals. Additionally, your hands and feet remain in fixed positions for long periods of time. During cold weather be sure to wear heavy gloves and thick wool socks to protect your hands and feet.

In Arizona rapid changes in weather conditions occasionally present serious problems for the unprotected bicyclist. Sometimes a rider is unable to reach shelter before a sudden change in the weather occurs. The rapid passage of a cold-front or the arrival of a line of thunderstorms can lower temperatures dramatically in a very short time. With frontal passage, too, strong winds may make pedaling an arduous task.

In summer, dust storms, common to some desert areas, and thunderstorms, common to higher elevations, are to be avoided if at all possible. Both are difficult to peddle through and during both visibility is diminished, making the possibility of accidents greater.

Weather is an important factor to be considered on even the shortest rides, but with proper preparations and commonsense bicycling can be enjoyed year-around in Arizona.

## EQUIPMENT: WHAT YOU NEED

THE BICYCLE

The ten-speed derailleur bicycle is the recognized standard for bicycle touring. It has dropped handlebars, a diamond-shaped frame, 27-inch wheels, caliper handbrakes, and a plastic or leather seat. The particular make and model is a matter of personal choice, but the better the bicycle the easier it is to ride and pedal.

Choosing a bicycle is like selecting an automobile. Cost, intended use, optional equipment, weight, color and manufacturer are all factors to be considered. Bicycles sold in department stores are not designed for touring, usually being too heavy and often poorly constructed and carelessly assembled.

A bicycle suited to the individual makes the pace easier, the hills less tiring and the road seem smoother. Specialized bicycle shops exist in most Arizona towns and these reputable dealers can offer advice and suggestions. In addition, more information can be obtained from experienced cyclists and bicycling publications.

Women as well as men should select the diamond-frame bicycle for extended riding and touring. Diamond-shaped frames, as opposed to women's or mixte's, are stronger, lighter and more responsive. Wheels should be made of an alloy rather than steel, for light-weight wheels make the pedals easier to turn—an important advantage on steep hills. Tires should be of the clincher type rather than the lighter "sew-ups," because they are less susceptible to punctures, are easier to fix on the road and are cheaper. The seat should be comfortable to a particular rider's

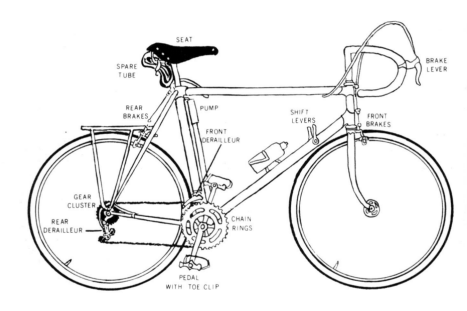

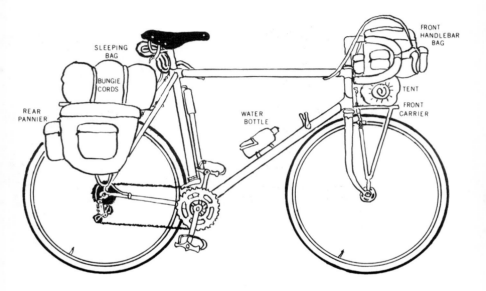

anatomy. If the original one is painful to sit on it can be replaced at a minimal cost from a wide variety, some of which are specifically designed for women. A good bicycle is not inexpensive, but a good one will last the owner a lifetime if it is properly cared for.

OPTIONAL EQUIPMENT

On other than neighborhood rides, a bicycle can be equipped with various accessories to make the task of pedaling easier and the ride more pleasant. To increase pedaling efficiency, toe clips and straps may be attached to the pedals. Learning to use these mechanical aids correctly takes time, but they increase pedaling efficiency by as much as twenty percent. They help smooth out the pedal stroke, enable a cyclist to keep his feet on the pedals without effort, and greatly aid in ascending steep hills by allowing the bicyclist to stand and "pump" to the top of the hill.

At first toe clips and straps feel awkward, but with practice they help the rider become one with the machine.

The addition of a pint water bottle, which can be attached directly to the frame, enables a thirsty rider to drink without stopping. Also, the water provides a margin of safety if the cyclist should be delayed far from home.

Tools for repairing flat tires are attachable directly to the bicycle. Underneath the seat, in a small specialized pouch or old sock, an extra tube, patch kit and tire irons can be carried, strapped to the seat rails. The tire pump is afixed directly to the frame.

CLOTHING

Over the years specialized clothing has been developed to aid the biker's passage down the road. The prime enemy of a cyclist is air resistance. Clothing is designed to be tight-fitting to cut resistance-- and it comes in bright colors so it can be seen more readily from a distance. Cycling jerseys have two or three pockets in the rear, for wallets, keys, food or other items.

Cycling shorts were originally black so they would

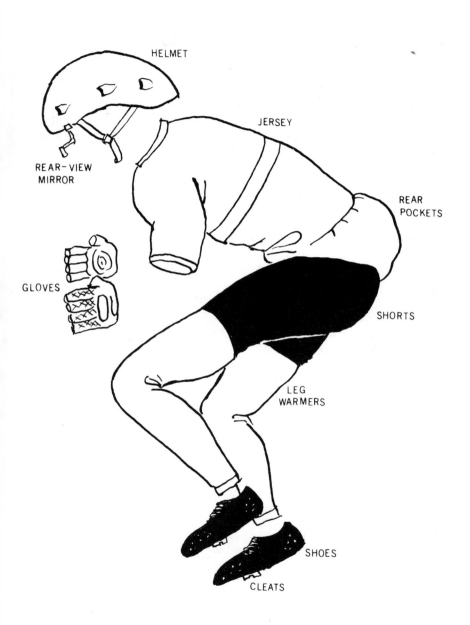

not show stains caused by the oil used to soften leather seats. The invention of plastic seats has elimin-
ated this problem and shorts now come in a variety of
colors. All come with a chamois sewn into the crotch
to add padding. They are designed to be worn without
underwear, and the chamois also serve to absorb sweat.

Shoes, with cleats attached to the soles, are designed to hold the feet firmly in position on the pedals when used in conjunction with toe clips and
straps. Although awkward to walk in, their use signi-
ficantly increases cycling ability.

Cycling gloves, with padded palm areas, help to cut
down road shock. Fingerless versions are available for
use during warm or hot weather.

Besides specialized clothing, there are additional
items worn for safety reasons. Light-weight helmets,
of impact-proof plastic or padded leather, have been
developed to protect the head in case of accident.
Tiny rearview mirrors that attach to sunglasses or
helmets help the rider see traffic behind.

For cold weather riding there are such things as
leg warmers--one for each leg--that are pulled on like
long socks and tucked underneath the cycling shorts.

TOURING EQUIPMENT

On short rides a cyclist needs only to carry the
tools necessary to fix flats, a water bottle or two
(depending on the season), and perhaps a snack tucked
into a jersey pocket. On other rides, however, a jacket, camera and a number of other small items may be
desired. These may be carried in a specially designed
bag that attaches to the handlebars. (These bags are
useful, but remember that even the smallest and light-
est one will affect the turning characteristics of
your bicycle.)

Rear carriers, attached to the frame, provide a
secure platform for carrying both light and heavy
loads. These carriers provide a more stable method of
transporting items, but keep in mind that whatever
you carry is susceptible to bumping and jarring. They
are also impossible to reach while riding. For this
reason it is preferable to carry cameras and other

valuables in front handlebar bags, using the rear carriers for heavier, bulkier items.

On overnight or longer tours, *panniers* are attachable to rear carriers. Panniers are like back-packs except they are made for bicycles. They enable the bicyclist to carry the same sort of equipment the backpacker carries.

By carefully selecting lightweight equipment, a biker can carry enough essentials and supplies to travel fully self-contained. With care, the weight of the gear needed for a weekend trip or even a journey of much longer duration can be kept in the 30-40 pound range.

The major difference between bicycle touring and backpacking is that a cyclist rarely has to carry more than small amounts of food. He can buy the bulk of his food as he needs it. This enables the touring cyclist to keep the weight of his supplies to a minimum.

Because touring subjects the bicycle to greater forces due to greater weight, and touring often takes the rider far from a repair shop,it is advisable to carry a repair kit. Here are two lists—the first one being the basic items needed for a tour of any length, and the second one being the tools one needs to repair most mechanical failures that may occur on the road.

BICYCLE: pump, rear carrier, handlebar bag, panniers, water bottles, lock and cable.

PERSONAL: helmet, sunglasses, rearview mirror, cycling shorts, jersey, cycling gloves, 1 short-sleeve shirt, 1 long-sleeve shirt, 1 pair long pants, 1 pair shorts, 2 pair socks, 1 pair underwear, wool sweater, windbreaker, rain parka or cape, running or cycle shoes, other pair sport shoes, towel.

FOR MOUNTAIN TRIPS: warm gloves or mittens, wool hat, warm vest or down jacket.

CAMPING: sleeping bag, ground cloth, foam pad or air mattress, tent with rain fly, stove and fuel, eating utensils (cup, bowl, spoon, knife).

MISCELLANEOUS: bungie cords (to tie down luggage).

suntan lotion, sewing kit, pocket knife, camera and film, toilet paper, map, flashlight, soap, matches, toothbrush and toothpaste.

FIRST-AID: adhesive bandages, adhesive tape, large gauze pads, small scissors, band-aids, antibacterial first-aid cream, antibacterial liquid soap, tweezers, lip balm, aspirin, upset stomach aid.

TOOLS & SPARE PARTS: tire irons, extra tubes, tube patch kit, adjustable wrench (6-inch), small screwdriver, pliers, extra spokes (5 or 6), freewheel remover (needed to remove gear cluster--a must if you have broken spokes on the freewheel side), electrical tape, extra metric nuts and screws in various sizes, brake cable, gear cable, chain lube, oil.

## ADDITIONAL SOURCES OF INFORMATION

The books, magazines and newspapers listed here provide additional information on different aspects of bicycling--from touring and racing to how to repair bicycles and physiological considerations.

*How to Ride a Bicycle Safely, Efficiently & Painlessly,* by Anita Notdurft-Hopkins. Phoenix Books/Publishers, Phoenix. The most comprehensive book available on the techniques as well as the psychology of bike riding, with special sections for parents.

*Bike Tripping Coast to Coast,* by Anita Notdurft-Hopkins. Contemporary Books Inc., Chicago. The mechanics and fun of bicycle touring fully explained.

*Richard's Bike Book,* by Richard Ballantine. Ballantine Books Inc., New York. A good basic manual on bicycle maintenance and enjoyment.

*Bicycling Magazine,* 33 E. Minor St., Emmaus, Pa. A monthly magazine with articles of general interest.

*Bike World,* 1400 Stierlin Rd., Mountain View, Cal. A bimonthly magazine with emphasis on the technical aspects of bicycling.

*Competitive Cycling,* P.O. Box 1069, Nevada City, Cal. A monthly newspaper covering bicycle racing.

*Delong's Guide to Bicycles and Bicycling*, by Fred Delong. Chelton Book Co., Radnor, Pa. All inclusive and exhaustive study of the art and science of bicycling.

*It's Easy to Fix Your Bike*, by John McFarlan. Follett Publishing Co., Chicago. Fully illustrated guide to repairing all makes and models of bikes.

*Bike Hiking*, by Steve Sherman. Doubleday & Co., Garden City, New York. A short easy to read guide to bicycle touring.

*Winning Bicycle Racing*, by Jack Simes. Henry Regnery Co. A guide to bicycle racing.

*Velo-News*, Box 1257, Brattleboro, Vt. A biweekly newspaper with news about bicycle racing.

PART II / THE RIDES

## RIDE CLASSIFICATIONS

SHORT RIDES

Rides in this section are along routes that can be completed in a few hours. Although many of the rides are over basically flat terrain, some of them ascend some of the lesser mountains in Arizona. All of these rides begin and end in or near Phoenix and Tucson. Good for beginning cyclists.

INTERMEDIATE RIDES

These routes are over a variety of terrain, and suitable for an athletic beginner or those with some biking experience. The rides begin at different locations throughout Arizona.

LONG RIDES

Rides in this section can be completed in less than one day by the experienced biking tourist. Others may prefer to do only a section of the rides, or take two days to complete the route as described. The routes begin at different locations around the state.

OVERNIGHT TOURS

Routes in this section consist of two-day trips to various scenic locations around the state. Most are suitable for novice as well as experienced bicyclists. Overnight trips for both wintertime and summertime camping have been selected.

EXTENDED TOURS

Four tours ranging in length from about 200 miles to over 500 miles are included in this section for the experienced bicycle/camping enthusiast. One of the routes is the cross-Arizona link in the famous *Trans-America Bicycle Trail*.

# THE RIDES

## Part I / SHORT RIDES

## Part II / INTERMEDIATE RIDES

THE RIDES (Continued)

## THE RIDES (Continued)

## Part IV / EXTENDED TOURS

PHOENIX AREA:

OTHER CITIES:

## MUMMY MOUNTAIN LOOP / PHOENIX (EAST CENTRAL)

*SYNOPSIS: This short loop lies mostly within the city limits of Phoenix. It follows a circular path around Mummy and Camelback Mountains.*

ROUND-TRIP: 15 miles. Part day. 1 to 2 hours. Approximate elevation gain-loss: less than 300-feet. Best day and time to ride: Saturdays, Sundays and holidays. Particularly beautiful after a winter rain storm.

This is a popular loop-ride for Phoenicians who like to bicycle early in the morning. For the most part the traffic is light, and the roads are wide enough with adequate shoulders. Along a section of Mockingbird Lane and East Lafayette Boulevard there is a designated bike path.

The route circles both Mummy and Camelback Mountains, providing glimpses of suburban life at its wealthiest. Interesting side-trips are available for those who like exploring by bicycle. Only the basic route is described here but those with time to spare will find various streets that end at different elevation levels on the two mountains.

The loop starts at the intersection of Camelback Road and North 44th Street (mile 0.0). Begin by proceeding north on 44th Street and follow it as it bends east and becomes McDonald Drive (1.0). When McDonald meets Tatum (1.5) turn left on Tatum and cross Lincoln Drive (2.0). Turn right onto Mockingbird Lane and follow it as it winds around Mummy Mountain, turns south and re-crosses Lincoln Drive (8.5).

After crossing Lincoln, Mockingbird Lane again meets McDonald (9.0). Turn west (right) onto McDonald and follow it for only 0.2 of a mile where you turn left (south) onto Casa Blanca (9.2). Follow Casa Blanca southward, cross Camelback Road (11.0). At this point Casa Blanca becomes 66th Street. Proceed on 66th to E. Lafayette (11.5) and turn right, following it west until it meets N. 44th Street, a short distance from the intersection of Camelback Road and 44th St., where the loop started.

MUMMY MOUNTAIN LOOP MAP

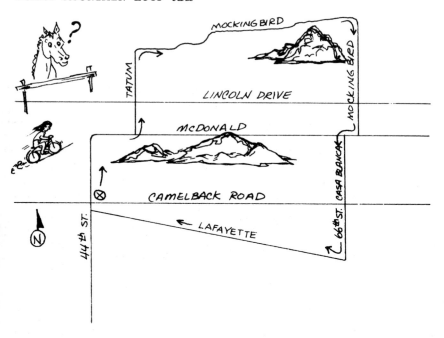

## SOUTH MOUNTAIN / PHOENIX (SOUTH CENTRAL)

*SYNOPSIS: The ride to the summit of South Mountain follows lightly traveled roads that are wholely with-in South Mountain Park--the largest city park in the nation. The expansive view of Phoenix and the sur-rounding desert from the top is the incentive for mak-ing the climb. There are moderate to severe grades on the way up the mountain.*

ROUND-TRIP: 23 miles. Part day. Allow 2 hours plus. Approximate elevation gain-loss: 1600 feet. Best day and time to ride: weekends and holidays, early in the morning. Light traffic on weekdays. Hot in summer.

South Mountain Park is a very large mountainous park adjoining Phoenix on the south. The ride provi-des a tour through typical desert vegetation only a short distance from downtown Phoenix. It involves a

steep climb and ends at an overlook which provides a
scenic view of the Valley of the Sun. It is one of
the most popular rides in the Phoenix area. The roads
are lightly traveled, except on weekend afternoons,
but one must be careful to avoid broken glass often
found near picnic and lookout parking areas. Spring
is of course the best season to see the desert in
bloom.

To reach the starting place for this ride, proceed
south on Central Avenue, two miles past Baseline Road,
where Central deadends at the park entrance. People
entering the park by car pay a 25¢ fee; bicylists may
enter free. Water bottles can be filled in the rest
rooms located at the entrance guard-house. Be sure to
park bicycles on the opposite side of the road from
the restroom facilties in the designated bike rack.

From the gate (mile 0.0), take the summit road for
1.5 miles to the first fork in the road. Here, you
may turn left and tackle the ascent without further
ado, but many prefer to first bear right and descend
to San Juan Lookout before returning and proceeding
toward the summit.

The 3-mile ride to San Juan Point (5.0) provides
a leisurely descent through typical desert flora. In
the spring, particularly after a heavy rain, yellow
poppies and other varities of wild flowers bloom
thickly along this section.

At San Juan turn around and retrace your path back
to the fork. This time bear right and proceed upward
another three miles to a second fork (12.0). Turning
left will take you, after a short steep climb, to Dobbins Point, where the best view of downtown Phoenix
is obtained.

To reach the summit, turn right at this junction
and proceed a mile to a third fork. The righthand
road leads to the television towers and Gila Valley
Lookout, the highest point on South Mountain (15.0).
The mile ride from the fork to Gila Valley Lookout
contains the steepest section of the ride.

Enjoy the view from the top before starting down.
Return via the same route, minus the detours (23.0)
Be especially careful on the descent.

SOUTH MOUNTAIN RIDE MAP

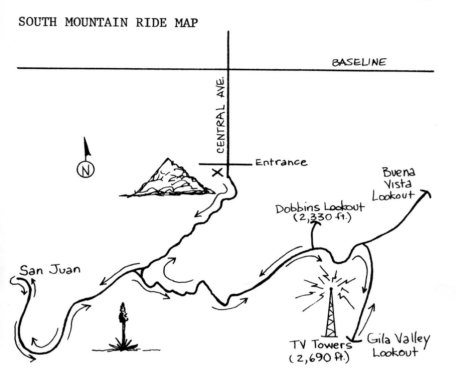

THUNDERBIRD PARK LOOP / NORTH PHOENIX

*SYNOPSIS: The first part of this flat loop is along a
well-traveled but wide Bell Road. The remainder is a-
long lightly traveled rural roads. Scenic Thunderbird
Park is about midway on the ride.*

ROUND-TRIP: 27 miles. Part day. Allow 2 to 3 hours.
Approximate elevation gain-loss: less than 500 feet.
Season: all year around; best in winter. Best day and
time to ride: anytime, although rush-hours should be
avoided.

The Thunderbird Park Loop provides a 27-mile ride
along flat roads just north of metropolitan Phoenix.
At midpoint, Thunderbird Park provides a scenic inter-
lude and a place to replenish water bottles. This ride
is at its best in winter, and is often used for early

season conditioning.

To reach the starting point from central Phoenix, proceed north on 7th Street until it intersects with Thunderbird Road (0.0). From here, proceed two miles north, still on 7th Street, to the intersection of 7th Street and Bell Road (2.0).

Turn left on Bell Road and continue on seven miles west to the intersection of Bell and 59th Avenue (9.0). Bell is often busy with traffic, but along this section it is a divided four-lane highway with adequate shoulders for safe bicycling.

At Bell Road and 59th Avenue, turn right onto 59th (9.0) and proceed north towards the mountains. Before reaching Thunderbird Park the road passes through orange groves.

After Thunderbird Park (11.0) the road goes up a short, steep hill. After going down the other side of the hill 59th turns east and becomes Pinnacle Peak Rd. (12.0). Four miles later Pinnacle Peak Road crosses the Black Canyon Freeway via an overpass (16.0). A mile further on it deadends at 19th Avenue (17.0). Turn right and proceed south for a mile to 19th Ave. and Deer Valley Road (18.0). Turn left on Deer Valley Road and pass Deer Valley Airport.

Just past the airport, Deer Valley Road intersects 7th St (20.0). From there return to the starting point via 7th Street (27.0).

## THUNDERBIRD PARK LOOP MAP

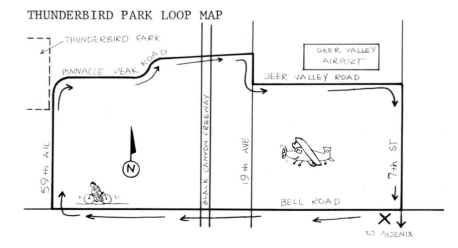

## LAKE PLEASANT / NORTHWEST PHOENIX

*SYNOPSIS: The focal point of this ride is Lake Pleasant, a large man-made lake northwest of Metro Phoenix. The ride features miles of basically flat terrain with typical desert vegetation. It is a good ride for bicyclist's to sample the desert without undue exertion.*

ROUND-TRIP: 40 miles. Part day. 3 to 4 hours. Elevation gain-loss: about 1000 feet. Season: late fall to early spring. Best day and time to ride: weekends during the early morning hours. At other times the traffic is usually light.

Lake Pleasant was formed by damming the Agua Fria River, and is a popular recreational area because of its proximity to Sun City, Glendale and Phoenix. The ride to and from the lake takes one through desert landscape, with little elevation change. The roads are wide, with good shoulders.

The starting point for this ride is at the intersection of Bell Road and North 99th Avenue, adjoining Sun City and 15 miles from downtown Phoenix. From the intersection (mile 0.0.) pedal north on N. 99th Ave. The terrain is flat with scrub desert vegetation.

After a few gentle hills you will reach the intersection of 99th Avenue (also called Lake Pleasant Rd.), and State Route 74. Turn left onto SR 74 and proceed west. After a few more undulating low hills you will arrive at the entrance road to Lake Pleasant (19.0). Turn right and go downhill a short distance before climbing back up to the park headquarters and the marina entrance (20.). Water and food are available.

Return via the same route.

A much longer loop ride can be made by continuing on to Morristown via SR 74. From Morristown take U.S. 60 back towards Phoenix. Highway 60 becomes Grand Avenue after it reaches Phoenix.

This makes a round-trip of about 55 miles. The terrain is similar to that encountered on the Lake Pleasant Road on the outward leg of the trip.

See map on the next page.

LAKE PLEASANT ROUTE MAP

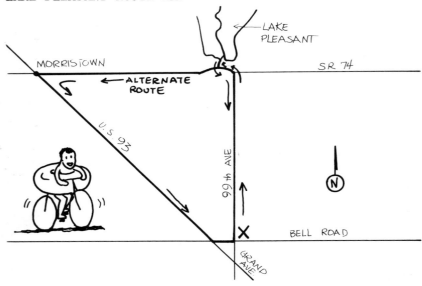

## SAGUARO LAKE LOOP / EAST PHOENIX, SCOTTSDALE
## TEMPE AND MESA

*SYNOPSIS: This loop ride takes the bicyclist into the foothills of Central Arizona's plateau country northeast of the Phoenix metropolitan area, and is one of the Valley's most popular rides for experienced bikers. It's a good circle of moderate length and difficulty. The desert-mountain scenery along the way is outstanding.*

ROUND-TRIP: 32 miles. Part day. Allow 3 to 4 hours. Approximate elevation gain-loss: 1500 feet. Season: all year, but hot and dry in summer. Best day and time to ride: weekends in the early morning; weekdays, anytime.

 The Saguaro Lake Loop parallels part of the Salt River that is particularly popular with inner-tubers, as it ascends into the foothills of mountains that stretch on and on. The outward loop highway is narrow and shoulderless,  but traffic is light in the early morning, the best time to ride.

To reach the starting point, proceed east on McKellips Road (from Scottsdale and Tempe) to the intersection of McKellips and Bush Highway, about 15 miles east of Scottsdale. From the intersection (0.0) proceed north on Bush Highway.

At McDowell Road (1.0), Bush Highway begins to run parallel to the Salt River. The section along the river features a number of low but steep hills in the vicinity of the Coon Bluff (8.0) turn-off.

The route then crosses to the other side of the Salt River via a bridge (12.0). The bridge often becomes submerged during winter flooding, and when it does the approaches usually wash out. Repetitive resurfacing has left the approaches uneven and bumpy. Cross with caution.

At the turn-off to Stewart Mountain Dam (14.0) the road bends sharply away from the river to ascend two steep grades leading to the entrance to Saguaro Lake Marina (16.0). Food and drinking water are available here.

The return route begins by heading back the same way as was traveled on the outward leg. At Bush Highway and Usuary Pass (22.0) turn left and immediately begin a moderate 3-mile climb to the flat summit of Usuary Pass (25.0).

There is hardly ever any traffic on this portion of the trip, and the beautiful saguaro cacti and palo verde trees make the climb especially worthwhile.

From the top of Usuary Pass (28.0) it is all downhill back to the starting point. Continue straight on Usuary Pass until you reach the MeKellips Road intersection (30.0). Turn right onto McKellips and continue on downhill to the intersection of McKellips and Bush Highway (32.0).

SAGUARO LAKE LOOP RIDE MAP

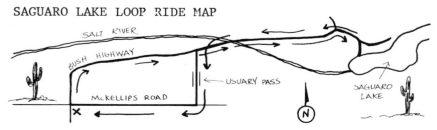

## "A" MOUNTAIN / CENTRAL TUCSON

*SYNOPSIS: This short ride ascends a Tucson landmark. From the summit of "A" Mountain (used as a lookout point by Indians and later Territorial soldiers) you have a fantastic panoramic view of Tucson and the sur-rounding country. The ride is all within the city lim-its of Tucson.*

ROUND-TRIP: 11 miles. Time required: 1-2 hours. Approx-imate elevation gain-loss: 800 feet. Season: all year. Best day and time to ride: any time except rush hours.

Although broken glass is often thick on the one-way loop section of this ride, it is popular because it is a short, steep climb, it is only minutes from down-town Tucson and the rewards are great.

The route begins at the intersection of Park Street and Speedway Boulevard (mile 0.0) adjacent to the Uni-versity of Tucson. Start by heading west on Speedway. This first section is usually crowded with cars, but most of the trip is along quiet backstreets, and is a good ride for beginners.

Proceed through the underpass beneath I-19 Freeway (2.0) and go on to the intersection of Speedway and Silverbell Road. Turn left onto Silverbell and go a little further to the junction of Silverbell and Cues-ta Ave. (4.0). Turn right onto Cuesta. After only a few blocks, Cuesta becomes Summit Peak Road. The one-way ascent up the mountain begins shortly (5.0) and winds its way up the summit of the cone-shaped moun-tain. Return via the same route (after descending by the one-way road going down). 11.0. Watch for glass.

"A" MOUNTAIN RIDE MAP

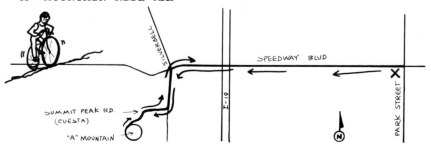

## SAN XAVIER MISSION / CENTRAL TUCSON

*SYNOPSIS: This flat ride leads to one of Arizona's oldest and best-known landmarks, the famous "White Dove of the Desert," originally built by Spanish missionaries. The church, now fully restored and in use by Papago Indians, was the site of Tucson's first European settlement.*

ROUND-TRIP: 32 miles. Time required: 2-3 hours. Elevation gain-loss: less than 300 feet. Season: all year. Best day and time: anytime; avoid rush hours.

This ride starts in central Tucson and winds around "A" Mountain before generally following the course of the Santa Cruz River (usually dry) to the mission's entrance. Most of the route is along narrow shoulderless country roads that carry a surprising amount of traffic despite the rural setting.

The trip begins at Park and Speedway (0.0.) next to the UofA. Head west on Speedway, go to Silverbell (3.0), and turn left onto Silverbell, following it around "A" Mountain. At the 5-mile mark Silverbell becomes Mission Road.

Continue on Mission Road and after crossing State Route 86 (6.0), go straight. A short while later, (13.0) Mission Road enters the San Xavier Indian Reservation. Mission Road connects with San Xavier Mission Road at the 16-mile mark, near the mission.

Return via the same route (32.0). Of, if you wish you may continue straight on San Xavier Mission Road. After crossing the Freeway turn left onto U.S. 89 for the return trip to downtown Tucson. This portion of U.S. 89 is heavily traveled, however, and once in Tucson you must use narrow city streets to get back to the UofA area. The distance via this alternate route is about the same (32.0).

See map on the next page.

SAN XAVIER MISSION RIDE MAP

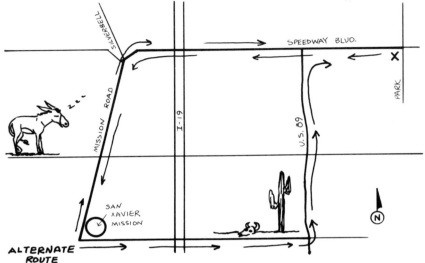

SABINO CANYON / EAST TUCSON

*SYNOPSIS: The trip up Sabino Canyon, one of the most beautiful canyons in Arizona, takes the biker into the confines of the spectacular Catalina Mountains. The most scenic portion of the trip is the last 3.7 miles, which is closed to motor vehicles. The ride is especially attractive in the spring when the stream flowing down the canyon is full and the surrounding area bright with new growth. This is a good ride for learning and perfecting hill-climbing techniques.*

ROUND-TRIP: 26 miles. Time required: 2-3 hours. Elevation gain-loss: about 1500 feet. Season: all year. Best day and time: anytime.

    Part of the approach route to Sabino Canyon has a bike lane along Sabino Canyon Road, making it safe for bicycling. The climb into the canyon is moderate with an occasional steep stretch.
    The starting point for the Sabino Canyon Ride is the intersection at Speedway and Wilmot (0.0), on Tucson's east side. Proceed north on Wilmot. At the

0.5 mark Wilmot meets Tanque Verde Road. Bear right on Tanque Verde and continue to the intersection of Tanque Verde and Sabino Canyon Rd. (2.0). Turn left on Sabino Canyon Road and begin a gentle descent.

The bike path begins after you cross El Cid (6.0). Follow it past the Sabino Canyon lower shuttle area (7.0) and continue to Lower Sabino Canyon (9.0).

From this point on motor vehicles are prohibited. Follow the road, which parallels the course of the stream, to the trail's end (12.7). Return via the same route, exercising caution on the descent (26.0).

SABINO CANYON RIDE MAP

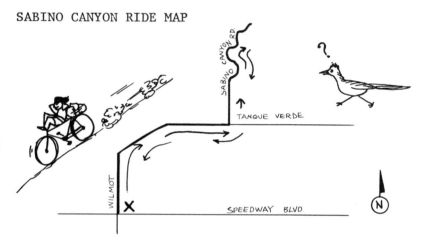

SKYLINE DRIVE / EAST TUCSON

*SYNOPSIS: This ride, across the flanks of the Catalina Mountains, provides panoramic views of Tucson from high vantage points. The roller coaster nature of much of the train makes it an exciting bicycling experience.*

ROUND-TRIP: 32 miles. Time required: 3-4 hours. Elevation gain-loss: 1400 feet. Season: all year; hot in the summer. Best day and time to ride: weekends, early in the morning.

Skyline Drive is one of Tucson's most picturesque streets. It runs east and west across the lower slopes

of the Catalina Mountains. Many washes have been cut
into the mountain slopes, and the ride dips in and out
of each of them.

This ride also begins at Speedway and Wilmot and
proceeds to just before the entrance to the lower
shuttle parking area of Sabino Canyon. Turn off of Sabino Canyon Road onto Sunrise Road (5.0). Continue
across Craycroft (8.0) to the junction of Sunrise Rd.
and Swan Road (9.0). Turn right onto Swan and go north
to Skyline Drive (10.0). Turn left onto Skyline Drive
and go through the roller-coaster section past Camp-
bell (12.0) to Ina Road (14.0). Turn left onto Ina
and continue on to the junction of Ina and Oracle Highway (16.0). This is the half-way point.

Return by the same route (32.0), or if you wish,
go south on Oracle to an east-west street that crosses
Tucson by a flatter route.

SKYLINE DRIVE ROUTE MAP

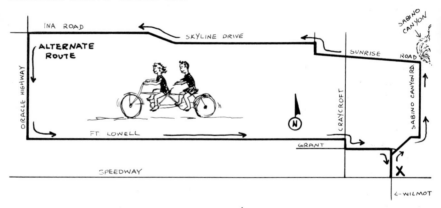

PINNACLE PEAK LOOP / CENTRAL PHOENIX

*SYNOPSIS: The ride to Pinnacle Peak from downtown
Phoenix provides the bicyclist with a view of Para-
dise Valley, one of the state's fastest growing areas.
North of Bell Road you pass through virgin desert.
The midpoint of the ride provides a scenic overview
of the desert. The return route passes through the
northern edge of Scottsdale.*

ROUND-TRIP: 46 miles. Part day. Allow 4-5 hours. Elevation gain-loss: 1200 feet. Season: winter and spring.
Best day and time to ride: weekends; early morning.

The Pinnacle Peak Loop is mostly a flat, circular
ride with one long moderate climb near the midpoint.
Part of the return leg is along the same route, but
this is the most scenic section of the ride--and it's
downgrade, always a delight.

The roads are wide on most of the route; in some
areas there are four lanes with good shoulders. Traffic can be heavy in the Scottsdale area. Unless the
trip is planned so you reach the midpoint when the
Pinnacle Peak area tourist attractions are open you
will have no place to refill your water bottles.

Starting point for the trip is Camelback Road and
44th Street. Head north on 44th. As it swings around
Camelback Mountain it becomes McDonald Drive (1.0).
At the intersection of McDonald and Tatum, turn left
onto Tatum (1.5) and go north, crossing Shea (6.0)
and Cactus (7.0), and continuing on to Bell Road
(10.0).

Turn right onto Bell and go east to Scottsdale
Road (13.0). Turn left onto Scottsdale Road and go
north to Pinnacle Peak Road (17.0). Turn right onto
Pinnacle Peak Road. From here it is a gradual seven
mile climb to Pinnacle Peak and the Reata Pass recreation area (24.0). The desert along North Scottsdale Road and Pinnacle Peak is much like it was hun-
dreds of years ago.

When ready to return, retrace the same route to
the Scottsdale Road intersection (35.0), turn left
and go south all the way to Camelback Road in the
center of Scottsdale. Turn right onto Camelback Road
and return to your starting point at 44th Street
(46.0).

See map on the following page.

## PINNACLE PEAK LOOP MAP

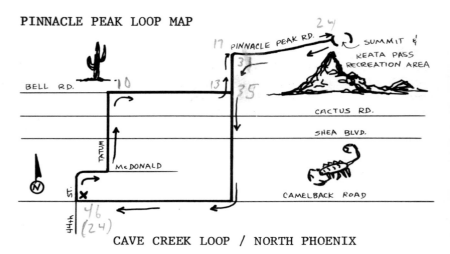

CAVE CREEK LOOP / NORTH PHOENIX

*SNYOPSIS: This long circle ride in the desert and foot-hills to the north of Metropolitan Phoenix takes you along the famous Desert Foothills Scenic Drive, one of the most attractive areas in Arizona. The loop swings through the former stage-coach town of Cave Creek, ad-joining the exclusive resort community of Carefree.*

ROUND-TRIP: 59 miles. Part day. Allow 4-6 hours. Elevation gain-loss: 1500 feet. Season: winter and early spring. Best day and time to ride: Sundays or holidays in the early morning.

This is a popular intermediate ride in the early spring for those who appreciate the desert in bloom. The tour also gives you an opportunity to visit the picturesque communities of Cave Creek and Carefree, both of which have several areas of special interest and good restaurants.

Most of the ride is along a two-lane road that is adequate and safe when the traffic is light. There is a gradual uphill climb on the outward swing, while the homeward section is a delightful downgrade roller-coaster run.

The ride begins at Camelback Road and 44th Street and follows the Pinnacle Peak Loop route to the intersection of Pinnacle Peak Road and Scottsdale Road

(17.0). Continue northward on Scottsdale Road.  Two
miles further on (19.) the Desert Foothills Scenic
Drive begins. Signs identify the different varieties
of cacti and other desert plants. The designated
scenic area continues to the outskirts of Cave Creek
and Carefree (25.0). Scottsdale Road ends when it encounters Cave Creek Road (27.0).

If you wish to explore the fabulous planned community of Carefree, turn right. It is just over a
rise. The loop swings left onto Cave Creek Road and
takes you south to the town of Cave Creek (28.),
with its picturesque shops and restaurants.  Leaving
Cave Creek, the route rises and falls as it emerges
from the foothills, taking you through the center of
the Cave Creek portion of the Desert Foothills Scenic
Drive.

The "roller-coaster" section of the highway ends
where Cave Creek Road crosses Dynamite Road (36.0).
The designated scenic drive ends two miles further on.
The rest of the return trip is a long gradual descent
into Phoenix via Cave Creek Road, which ends at the
intersection of 7th Street and Dunlap (50.0).

Continue south on 7th Street to Glendale Ave.,
turn east on Glendale and go to 24th Street, turn
right and go to Camelback Road, turn left and return
to your original starting point at 44th St. (59.0).

CAVE CREEK LOOP MAP

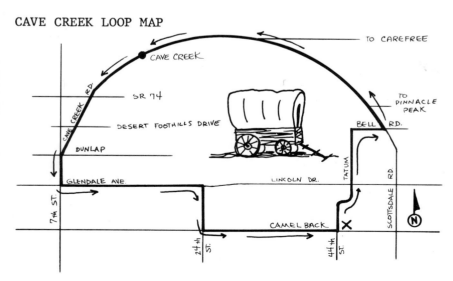

## FOUNTAIN HILLS LOOP / EAST PHOENIX

*SYNOPSIS: This is one of the most interesting and pop-
ular rides in the Metro Phoenix area, combining fascinating desert and foothill scenery, spectacular
views of Scottsdale, Mesa and the Mountains, a visit
to a remarkable planned community and crossing part
of an Indian Reservation.*

ROUND-TRIP: 45 miles. Part day. Allow 3-5 hours. Elevation gain-loss: 1200 feet. Season: spring and fall.
Best day and time to ride: weekends and holidays;
early morning or late afternoon.

   This tour also starts at Camelback Road and 44th
Street (a favorite staring point). Go north on 44th
and McDonald to Tatum, proceed on Tatum to Shea
Blvd. (6.0). Turn right onto Shea, going east. Shea
widens before it reaches Scottsdale Road (9.0). Continue on across Scottsdale Road, Hayden Road (10.0)
and Pima Road.
   At the 14-mile mark you reach the Taliesin West
turn-off. This is a large living complex built by
Frank Lloyd Wright as a winter residence and now used
as a school for architecture students. Guided tours
of the picturesque complex are available if you want
to make a side trip.
   The ride continues eastward, however, and soon begins a long gradual climb. Near the summit (19.0),
the grade steepens. From the summit you have spectacular views of Four Peaks and the Mesa/Apache Junction
portion of the Valley of the Sun. From the summit it
is downhill to the Fountain Hills turn-off and the
intersection of Shea Blvd. with Bee Line Highway (SR
87) at the 23-mile mark.
   Here again you may want to take a side-trip into
Fountain Hills, one of the most beautiful planned
communities in the state. The ride turns right at Bee
Line Highway and heads south, shortly thereafter entering the Ft. McDowell Indian Reservation.
   At the intersection of Bee Line Highway and McDowell Road, turn right again and head west (34.0).

Continue on across Hayden Road (38.0) and Scottsdale
Road (39.0) to the intersection of McDowell and 68th
St. (40.). Turn right onto 68th St and proceed north
to a short distance beyond Indian School Road (42.5)
where you turn left onto Lafayette Blvd. Follow Lafayette west to 44th St., only a few yards from where
you started (45.0).

FOUNTAIN HILLS LOOP MAP

THE SOUTH MOUNTAIN LOOP / SOUTH PHOENIX

*SYNOPSIS: This ride around South Mountain takes you
into rural farmland just south of the Valley of the
Sun's highest mountain. Part of the route is along a
bike path paralleling the Western Canal.*

ROUND-TRIP: 46 miles. Time required: 3-4 hours. Elevation loss-gain: less than 300 feet. Season: late fall
or early spring. Best day and time: any time.

Besides offering views of South Mountain from all
sides, this route passes St. John's Mission, now an
Indian School, and one of the earliest settlements in
the Phoenix area. The roads are fairly wide and the
shoulders adequate. Once through Guadalupe traffic is

rare. Places to fill water bottles are few and far between.

Starting point for this ride is at Baseline Road
and 56th Street in Tempe, near the I-10 Baseline Exit.
From here (0.0) proceed south on 56th Street through
Guadalupe (1.0), past Williams Field Road (5.0), to
Beltline Road (11.0).

Turn right onto Beltline, a straight flat run through sage-covered desert that gradually swings into an
arc around the base of South Mountain. The St. John's
Mission turn-off is at the 21-mile mark near the
southwest corner of South Mountain. Just beyond the
mission, Beltline becomes South 51st Avenue.

Proceed on 51st Avenue to Dobbins Road (also called Laveen Road) and turn right onto Dobbins. Continue
eastward on Dobbins, cross Central Avenue (39.0) and
go on to 7th Street (40.0). Turn left and go to Western Canal. Turn right onto the designated bike path
that follows the canal as it winds its way eastward.

The bike path ends just short of 48th Street and
Baseline Road (45.0). Continue east on Baseline Road,
pass beneath I-10 and proceed on to your starting
point at 56th Street (46.0).

SOUTH MOUNTAIN LOOP MAP

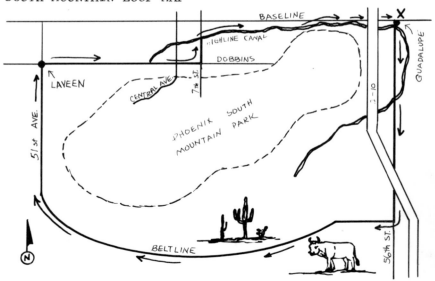

## TORTILLA FLAT / APACHE JUNCTION

*SYNOPSIS: Between Labor Day and Memorial Day a group of Phoenix-based bicyclists meet every Saturday morning in Apache Junction to ride to Tortilla Flat. The rigors of this route, the scarcity of traffic and the fantastic scenery along the way have made this one of Arizona's most popular bicycle rides.*

ROUND-TRIP: 36 miles. Part day. Allow 3-4 hours. Approximate elevation gain-loss: 1800 feet. Best day and time to ride: Saturday, shortly after sunrise.

Tortilla Flat is a tiny settlement in the foothills overlooking Apache Junction. It boasts a restaurant, a post office, general store and motel. So it is obviously its location in the always fascinating Superstition Mountains that attracts bikers; not its amenities.

Starting point for the trip is the parking lot of the Superstition Inn, located at the junction of U.S. 60 and State Route 88 (the famous Apache Trail), in Apache Junction, 25 miles east of Phoenix. From the Inn (0.0) you follow SR 88 for the entire trip. Traffic is usually light, but be wary of cars pulling boat-trailers on  some of the tighter curves. The steep graded downhills that make the ride exciting require both constant attention and a moderate degree of bicycling skill.

The Lost Dutchman State Park is at the 5-mile mark. Next  is Goldfield (7.0), followed by a Lookout (8.0) from which you have a breathtaking view of Weaver's Needle (believed by many to hold the key to finding the Lost Dutchman Gold Mine). From here, the road begins a steep climb into the foothills.

At the top of the second rise (11.0) another Lookout provides a good view of Four Peaks. These are often snowcapped in winter and provide a dramatic contrast with the brown desert mountains.

The trail now begins a steep descent to the edge of Canyon Lake, an island of blue in a sea of brown. The last turn before the lake requires extreme caution, as does the bridge that comes up shortly thereafter (13.0).

For the next few miles the road twists and turns along the edge of Canyon Lake, before crossing a second bridge over an arm of the lake (15.0). One more steep climb remains before you reach Tortilla Flat (18.0).

Adventurous bicyclists may wish to lengthen their ride by continuing five miles further on to where the pavement turns to dirt on the way to Roosevelt Lake. To do so, cross Tortilla Flat Creek, over which water flows after winter rains, and ascend a long, steep hill. It finally levels out shortly before turning to dirt at the 23-mile mark.

Return to Apache Junction via the same route.

THE TORTILLA FLAT RIDE MAP

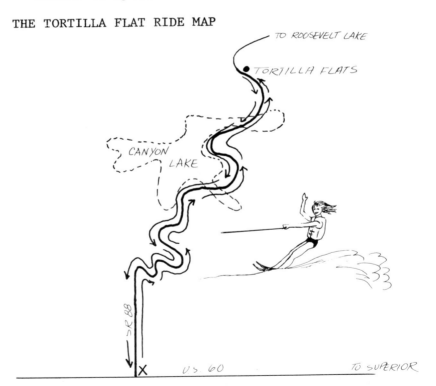

# SOME FASCINATING FACTS
## ABOUT ARIZONA

Inhabited by several Indian tribes for at least 20,000 years, first explored by the Spanish in 1539 A.D. and first visited by Americans in the 1820s, Arizona is a land of contrasts and superlatives.

The 6th largest state in the union (all of New England and most of New York state would fit nicely within its borders), Arizona has:

More parks and national monuments than any other state; more mountainous country than Switzerland; more sunshine than Florida; more golf courses than Scotland; the largest Indian population in the United States; the largest number and the largest percentage of Indian reservations in the country (19, incorporating 19,500,000 acres)...

Also, the largest Ponderosa pine forest in the world; the U.S.'s southernmost ski resort; the largest solar telescope in the world; the largest retirement community in the country; more cacti than anywhere else in the world; the largest known dry cave...and more.

Arizona's motto is *DITAT DEUS* or "God Enriches"--and it is easy to understand why.

The name "Arizona" is derived from the Indian words "Aleh Zon," which means "Little Spring" (the Spanish were already pronouncing it "Arizona" as early as 1736).

Arizona became a territory in 1863 (the bill was signed by Abraham Lincoln) and a state in 1912.

Cattle and cowboys are still very much a part of the everyday scene in Arizona, with 70 percent of the state's approximately 114,000 square miles of land devoted to grazing.

## COLOSSAL CAVE / EAST TUCSON

*SYNOPSIS: This scenic route is over rolling desert terrain, and is one of Tucson's most popular rides. The route approaches Saguaro National Monument East, where an interesting side trip is available. In addition, the section within Tucson is along a bike trail that parallels the famous Old Spanish Trail.*

ROUND-TRIP: 34 miles. Time required: 2-4 hours. Elevation gain-loss: less than 1100 feet. Season: all year; hot in summer. Best day and time to ride: weekends and holidays; early a.m.

Tucson was one of the first Western cities to construct bike paths, and the portion of this one that runs alongside of the Old Spanish Trail was one of the city's first bikeways.

The bike path takes up the first six miles of the ride. The last 11 miles is along a narrow, shoulderless road. Traffic is usually light, but many drivers are unfamiliar with the frequent ups and downs and twists in the road, so bicyclists must remain on the lookout. Water is available at both Saguaro National Monument and Colossal Cave.

The route begins at the intersection of Broadway and Old Spanish Trail (0.0) on the extreme east side of Tucson. Proceed east on the bike path beside Old Spanish Trail, cross Caino Seco (1.0) and Harrison (3.0). The terrain is gently rolling, and the houses  fewer the further you ride.

Still on the bike path, cross Houghton Road (5.0) and continue on to the entrance to Saguaro National Monument East (6.0). The bike trail ends here. You may make an interesting side trip into the monument, which has over 10 miles of well-maintained lightly traveled roads winding around among the giant cacti.

The route to Colossal Cave (the largest known dry cave in the world) continues straight on Old Spanish Trail. From this point to the cave there are no major intersections. The terrain becomes more rolling as you gradually climb onto the flanks of the Rincon Mountains.  A short, steep ascent into the cave park-

ing lot marks the half-way point (17.0). Return by
the same route. This ride is recommended for bicylists
of all ability.

COLOSSAL CAVE RIDE MAP

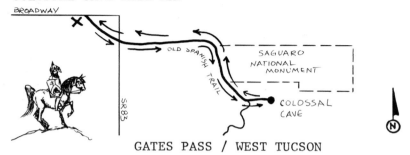

GATES PASS / WEST TUCSON

*SYNOPSIS: The Gates Pass ride takes you from downtown
Tucson into the desert west of the city by the most
direct route. After passing close to Old Tucson, a
reconstructed frontier town often seen in movies, the
route loops around the Arizona-Sonora Desert Museum,
where the marvels of desert ecology are explained
through realistic exhibits.*

ROUND-TRIP: 36 miles. Time: 3-5 hours. Elevation
gain-loss: 2000 feet. Season: all year; hot in summer. Best day and time to ride: anytime except during
rush hours.

    The route over Gates Pass is popular not only be-
cause it is extraordinarily scenic but also because
it goes to three of Arizona's most populr tourist
attractions: the Arizona-Sonora Desert Museum; Old
Tucson and Saguaro National Monument West. Besides
stopovers at Old Tucson and the desert museum, interesting side trips are available within the boundaries
of the fascianting forest of saguaro cacti.
    The streets within Tucson are usually busy with
traffic, and most of the roads on the route are narrow and shoulderless, so caution is necessary, especially on the steep sections of Gates Pass.
    The route begins at Park Avenue and Speedway Blvd.
(0.0) near the University of Arizona. Begin by head-

ing west on Speedway. Go under the Freeway (2.0),
pass Silverbell (3.0), the entrance to Pima Community
College (5.0), and continue on. After you pass Camino
de Oesta (6.0) Speedway becomes Gates Pass Road, and
this is where the real climb up to the top of the
pass begins.

On the way up there are great views of saguaros
which grow thickly on both sides of the narrow, steep
road. Tucson Mountain Park (9.0) begins just short of
the summit (10.0).

Descending the west side of the pass you come to
Kinney Road (12.0). The entrance to Old Tucson is a
few hundred yards south of the intersection. To reach
the Arizona Desert Museum turn right on Kinney Road.
The entrance is three miles further on (15.0).

Going on past the museum entrance you come to the
junction of Kinney and McCain Loop Road (16.0), just
before the entrance of the saguaro monument. Turn
left onto McCain Loop Road. This will take you on a
short interesting loop-ride through the monument.

Return over Gates Pass Road to Speedway and Anklam
Road (26.0). Turn right onto Anklam and climb over a
long ridge. At Anklam and 6th Street (34.0) turn left
onto 6th Street and continue north to Speedway (35.0).
Turn right onto Speedway and proceed to your starting
point (36.0).

## GATES PASS ROUTE MAP

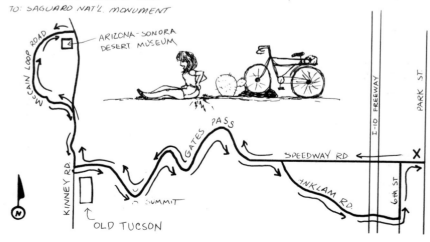

## PRESCOTT - SKULL VALLEY
### LOOP

*SYNOPSIS: The 51-mile Prescott-Skull Valley Loop provides a scenic view of high meadowland and tall pines. A visit to Prescott, a cattle and farming-oriented town in the world's largest stand of Ponderosa pines is an adventure within itself. Its a cool 5,350 ft.up.*

ROUND-TRIP: 51 miles. Time required: 4-5 hours. Approximate elevation gain-loss: 1800 feet. Season: late spring to early fall. Best day and time to ride: anytime.

This circular route provides you with an opportunity to visit the communities of Kirkland, Skull Valley and Nowhere, in addition to Prescott, which is the county seat of Yavapai County and 100 miles northwest of Phoenix.

The town square of Prescott has changed little since before the turn of the century, and it is a fascinating place to explore. Skull Valley and Kirkland are ranching communities, and Nowhere is not much more than a store and bar. The roads on the route are lightly traveled, and wide enough for safe bicycling.

Starting point is the town square in Prescott. Take U.S. 89 southward (0.0), which will quickly bring you to a long ascent to the "Top of the Pines" summit at an altitude of 6,000 feet (8.0). Continue on U.S. 89 out of the pines via a descent marked by numerous hairpin curves and occasional switchbacks.

The road straightens out into a long gradual downhill that passes Nowhere (14.0) before encountering Kirkland Junction (20.0) at the bottom of the downgrade. Turn right onto State Route 96. At Kirkland (24.0) turn right again onto SR 255, just after the railroad tracks, which must be negotiated with care.

The return trip to Prescott follows SR 255 all the way. From Kirkland the return is mostly uphill. Outside of Kirkland the road crosses a series of steep but fairly short hills before passing Skull Valley (31.0), located just off the main highway. Water is available in a small general store.

After a lengthy traverse of a ridge, the road gradually steepens for the climb back into the pines to Prescott. Part of the climb is very steep, but after Iron Springs (43.0) the ascent moderates and the pines reappear. From the summit (48.), which is 5,920 feet high, its a short 3-mile descent back to your starting point (51).

PRESCOTT-SKULL VALLEY ROUTE MAP

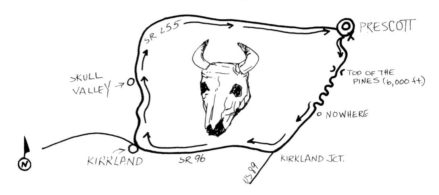

## WUPATKI MONUMENT LOOP
## FLAGSTAFF

*SYNOPSIS: This trip offers an opportunity to visit prehistoric Indian homesites as well as an ice cave and Sunset Crater, one of the most spectacular extinct volcanoes in northern Arizona.*

ROUND-TRIP: 51 miles. Part day: allow 6 hours. Elevation loss-gain: 2,500 ft. Season: Late spring through early fall. Best day and time to ride: anytime.

The Wupatki National Monument Loop encompasses both typical high mountain and high plateau scenery. Within the monument area are over 800 ancient Indian homesites and numerous volcanic features, all of which have been carefully preserved.
Part of the route is along U.S. 89, which is a major highway carrying considerable traffic. It has

good shoulders that offer safe bicycling, but caution
is urged. The remainder of the route is over the monument road which is very lightly traveled except in
the area of Sunset Crater. The monument road surface,
however, is often rough and potholed.

Except for an occasional Indian trading post on
U.S. 89 there are no food or water facilities on this
circular route.

Starting point is the Visitor Center (0.0) on the
monument road, three miles off of U.S. 89 (monument
road branches off of the main highway 20 miles north
of Flagstaff. Begin the loop by heading back through
the tall pines and across a high meadow toward U.S.
89 (3.0). Turn right onto the highway. From here to
the northern entrance to the monument it is 15 miles
and a drop in elevation of 2,500 feet. On the rapid
descent the scenery changes from pine and mountain
meadow to typical high plateau country scrub brush.

At the northern entrance to the monument (18.0)
turn right onto the monument road, which heads a-
cross scrub range land. Indian ruins dot the occasional hilltops. Signs explain how the Indians lived
and what the various buildings were used for.

Gradually the barren landscape changes to scrub
pines as the road rises and enters the volcanic sections of the monument (30.0). After a steep climb you
reach the high point before Sunset Crater (40.0) and
then seven miles further on the crater itself. The
Visitor Center reappears on the 51st mile.

WUPATKI MONUMENT LOOP MAP

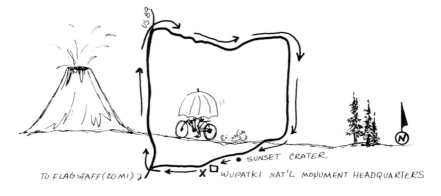

US 89

SUNSET CRATER

TO FLAGSTAFF (20 MI)      X  WUPATKI NAT'L MONUMENT HEADQUARTERS

## TEMPE - CASA GRANDE LOOP

*SYNOPSIS: This ride begins in Tempe, passes through the Indian settlement of Sacaton on the way to Casa Grande, and returns to Tempe via the farming community of Maricopa. It is a long but easy ride over mostly flat terrain in Central Arizona's "Golden Corridor."*

ROUND-TRIP: 93 miles. Time required: 6-7 hours. Elevation loss-gain: less than 400 feet. Season: late fall to early spring. Best day and time: any time except windy (or rainy!) days.

This is a popular fall, winter and early spring ride that is long but not taxing. The roads are sufficently wide to provide for safe bicycling. Traffic is normally light on all sections.The towns are far apart, however, so water bottles should be filled at each existing opportunity.

Starting point is at Rural and Baseline Roads in south Tempe (0.0). Proceed east on Baseline, pass Dobbins Road (3.0) and Alma School Road (4.0) to where Baseline meets State Routes 87 and 93, which run together (5.0). Turn right and proceed south on SRs 87/93.

Just south of Chandler (mile 10.0) the two routes divide (18.). Follow SR 93 toward Interstate 10 (the Freeway). Immediately before the I-10 overpass turn left onto Casa Blanca Road (24.0). Do not cross over the freeway.

It is a flat six miles from here into Sacaton (30.0). Turn right at the first unsigned intersection in Sacaton (30.0), where there is a stop sign. A mile further on turn right again at another unsigned road (31.0). There is a sign pointing toward Casa Grande. Ascend the only hill on the entire trip, and turn right onto SR 93 (37.0), cross I-10 at mile 38.0 and proceed on into Casa Grande, the half-way point of the trip.

To return, turn right off of SR 93 onto Cottonwood Lane (45.0), and ride through a long section of flat, brush and tumbleweed covered desert. At the small

town of Maricopa (67.0) Cottonwood Lane runs into
Maricopa Road. Turn right onto Maricopa Road and go
north. After crossing the Gila River (75.0) you re-
enter Maricopa County (77.0) before passing Firebird
Lake (83.0).

Maricopa Road now becomes S. 56th Street. Continue
north on S. 56th, cross Williams Field Road (85.0),
and pass through the Yaqui Indian village of Guadalupe (90.0). At the intersection of 56th Street and
Baseline Road, turn right onto Baseline and travel
the last two miles to your starting point (93.0).

Much of this trip is on the Gila River Indian
Reservation.

TEMPE-CASA GRANDE LOOP MAP

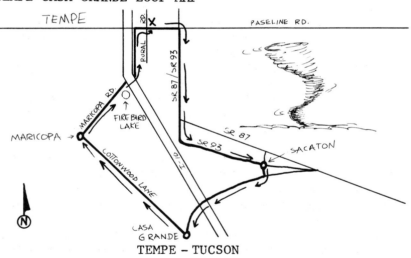

TEMPE – TUCSON

*SYNOPSIS: There is an especially scenic route between
Tempe and Tucson that is particularly suited to bicycle travel. This is the famous Pinal Pioneer Parkway,
which passes through one of the most beautiful desert
areas in the state, and has a minimum of auto traffic.*

ONE-WAY: 121 miles. Time required: 1 day. Elevation
gain-loss: 1,000 feet. Season: late fall to early
spring. Best day and time to ride: any time; but an
early morning start is best.

Traveling by bicycle between Metro Phoenix and Tucson, Arizona's two largest cities, is more popular than one might think. Among other things, a Phoenix radio station sponsors an annual Phoenix to Tucson ride, and the University of Arizona sponsors the annual Camp Wildcat Bike-A-Thon from Tucson to Tempe to raise money for handicapped children.

The Tempe-Tucson ride avoids all large towns, and for the most part the terrain is flat. In some areas it is necessary to go off the route slightly to obtain water.

Starting point for the trip is at Rural and Baseline Roads in south Tempe, near the I-10 Freeway Baseline Exit. From here (0.0) head west on Baseline to State Route 87/93 (5.0). Turn right on SR 87/93 and continue south through Chandler (10.0) and on to where SR 87 and 93 split (18.0). Bear left on SR 87 and proceed toward Coolidge. You will soon enter the Gila River Indian Reservation.

Continue on past the SR 187 turn-off (32.0) and the SR 387 turn-off (36.0) to the junction of SR 87 and 287 (43.0). Bear left on 287 toward Florence until it intersects with U.S. 80/89 (52.0). Follow U.S. 80/89 south.

Shortly beyond this junction you enter the Pinal Pioneer Parkway, the famous scenic desert route that has signs naming the different desert plants (65.0), and pass a memorial to Tom Mix, killed there in a 1-car crash in 1940.

Just beyond a power relay station (91.0) you begin a gradual descent to Oracle Junction (95.0). Continue on U.S. 80/89 through tiny Catalina (99.0), past Canon de Oro (106.0) and Ina Road (112.0), which marks the outskirts of Tucson. Continue on U.S. 80/89 straight to Main Street (119.0). Go one block on Main Street to Speedway Blvd., and turn left on Speedway. Go east to Park Avenue, next to the UofA.

Map on following page.

## TEMPE-TUCSON ROUTE MAP

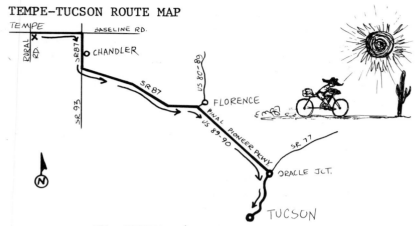

## MT. LEMMON / EAST TUCSON TOUR

*SNYOPSIS: The ascent of Mt. Lemmon provides a bicycle adventure up Arizona's highest paved road (summit: 9,157 feet). The route takes the cyclist, in a few hours of hard pedaling, from the low Sonora desert to high pine forests. Suitable for experienced, well-conditioned bicyclists.*

ROUND-TRIP: 70 miles. Part day: allow 5-6 hours. Elevation gain loss: 7,000 feet. Season: late spring to early fall. Best day and time: Avoid weekends and holidays if possible.

The ride begins on the outskirts of Tucson and ends at the base of the ski slope, high on Mt. Lemmon. The road is narrow with no shoulders. Traffic can be very heavy at times, and in some areas cars may bunch up behind a bicyclist because passing is difficult.

Starting point is at Speedway and Wilmot (0.0) on Tucson's east side. Proceed north on Wilmot to where it meets Tanque Verde Road (0.5). Bear right onto Tanque Verde and continue across Sabino Canyon Road (2.0). Follow Tanque Verde as it bends to the north to cross Tanque Verde Wash (3.0). At Catalina Highway (4.0) turn left onto the highway.

The gradual descent which has marked the journey so far now levels off as if to pause before beginning

a gradual rise to the base of Mt. Lemmon (9.0). The
climb begins in earnest at this point. After a series
of switchbacks through typical desert terrain you
reach the Molina Basin Camping Area (14.0), where
junipers and other small pines begin to appear. By
the time you reach Bear Canyon Camping Area (23.0)
the desert has been left far below, and you are near
big pine country.

The stretch from Bear Canyon to Windy Point (25.0)
is the steepest of the trip. From here on the grade
is more gradual and the pines profuse. Continue past
the Palasades area, where a U.S. Forest Service office is located. It is cool now and you have another
2,000 feet of vertical climbing.

Continue on to the Summerhaven Recreation Area
(33.0), where there are cabins, shops and a general
store. Shortly beyond, the pavement ends at the entrance to the U.S.'s southernmost ski resort (35.0).

Descending Mt. Lemmon requires extreme caution.
The grade and washboard nature of the road surface
combine to make the descent hazardous. Strength and
stamina are required to keep pressure on the hand
brakes almost continuously. You must keep your speed
down and your bicycle under control at all times.
Return to the starting by the same route (70.0).

MT. LEMMON RIDE MAP

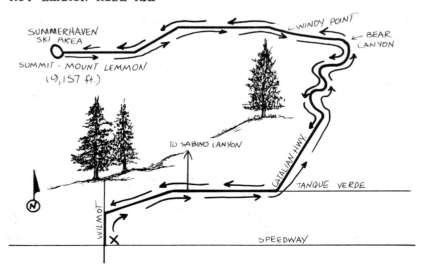

## KITT PEAK / TUCSON

*SYNOPSIS: Kitt Peak is the home of the internationally famous National Observatory, which houses some of the world's largest telescopes and is very important in mankind's study of the universe. The long ride takes one across nearly flat desert to the base of Kitt Peak and a spectacular ride to the 6,875-foot high summit. Much of this ride is on the Papago Indian Reservation.*

ROUND-TRIP: 92 miles. Full day: allow 6 to 8 hours. Elevation gain-loss: 5,000 feet. Season: early fall to late spring. Best day and time: Any day except Sunday (when the Observatory is closed). Plan to arrive between 10 a.m. and 3 p.m.

The Observatory is open to visitors from 10 a.m. to 4 p.m., six days a week. The desert portion of this ride is across vast open plains ringed by distant mountains. The 9-mile climb up Kitt Peak is steady, and steep in places.

Traffic on State Route 86, the main highway into the heartland of the huge Papago Indian Reservation, is usually light...but it can be busy in the early morning. It is fairly narrow most of the way and does not have shoulders.

Starting point is at Park Avenue and Speedway (0.0). Proceed west on Speedway to Silverbell, turn left and follow Silverbell/Mission Road to SR 86 (6.0). Turn right onto 86 and head out across the desert. Continue past Three Points (24.0) to the Kitt Peak Access Road (SR 386) at mile-37. Turn left and begin the ascent to the peak (46.0). Return via the same route (92.0). Take plenty of water.

KITT PEAK RIDE MAP

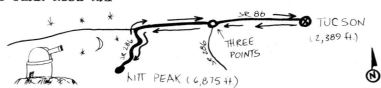

## MINING COUNTRY LOOP
## (SUPERIOR)

*SYNOPSIS: This 93-mile loop in east central Arizona
is noted for its steep climbs and views of copper
mines and smelters. It is a demanding ride for experienced riders.*

ROUND-TRIP: 93 miles. All day: 6-9 hours. Elevation
gain-loss: 6,800 feet. Best time to ride: mid or late
spring, and early or mid-fall. Note: Many riders prefer to make this a 2-day journey.

The long climbs, on the edge of the desert, make
this trip too hot in summer; and the long descents
make it too cold in winter. April is the best month,
when the desert hills are covered with wild flowers
in bloom.

The Mining Country Loop was pioneered by bicycle
racers seeking a demanding circular route of about
100 miles. It is raced every April by leading bike
racers, and is one of the most difficult century
rides in the U.S. Besides the challenges, the beautiful scenery also make it a favorite among Arizona
cyclists.

The ride starts and ends in Superior, a mining
town 50 miles east of Phoenix in the foothills at
an altitude of 2,830. Leave Superior (0.0) on U.S.
60 and head for Queen Creek Tunnel and the "Top of
the World" summit; elevation 4,615. Descend rapidly
past Blue Bird Copper Mine to Miami (26.). Continue
on U.S. 60 into Globe (34.0) and take the bypass,
just    beyond the railroad overpass, that leads to
the intersection of U.S. 60 and State Route 77.

Before leaving Globe fill your water bottles
and buy snacks, because its a long way to the next
services. Turn onto SR 77 and ascend El Capitan Pass
(el. 5,000) and then enjoy the 3,000-ft descent past
the Christmas Mine and on into Winkleman (50.) Here
there are motels and restaurants for those who wish
to stay overnight. There are no camping facilities.
From Winkleman (el. 1,938) follow SR 177 toward

Superior. Pass through Kearny and then begin a 5-mile 1,800 feet climb. Pass the Ray Copper Mine and proceed on to the "End of the World" summit (3,660-ft). The last mile of this climb is very steep. From the summit you can see Weaver's Needle, supposedly a marker for locating the legendary Lost Dutchman's Gold Mine. From here it is an easy 8-mile downhill ride to Superior (93.0).

## MINING COUNTRY RIDE MAP

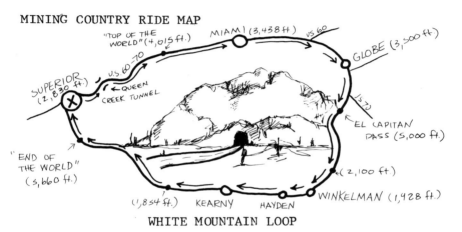

WHITE MOUNTAIN LOOP

*SYNOPSIS: This circle ride in northeastern Arizona's high country takes you through the heart of the White Mountain Recreation Area. It is a country of tall pines, towering peaks in the distance and mile-after-mile of unspoiled views of nature at its best.*

ROUND-TRIP: 104 miles. Full day: allow 7-8 hours, or two days if you prefer a leisurely pace. Elevation gain-loss: 3,000 feet. Season: summer or early fall. Best day and time: any time.

The ride starts in Showlow (el. 6,330-ft.) some 180 miles northeast of Phoenix. From Showlow (0.0) proceed east on U.S. 60 across a rolling prairie plateau to Springerville (45.0). Although U.S. 60 is a main east-west highway, traffic is usually light and the shoulders are adequate for cycling safely.

At Springerville turn right onto SR 260 and go west toward the Sunrise Ski Resort, which is a short distance off of 260, and an interesting side-trip. Shortly after you leave Springerville the road begins a steep ascent into the White Mountains. At the summit (el. 9,040) you are in heavily forested hills broken now and then by alpine meadows.

Once passed the Sunrise Ski Area turn-off (55.0) the road flattens out and begins a long gradual descent into Pinetop. The road along this section is narrow, but the traffic is usually light.

If you prefer to make this a 2-day trip you may want to stop at camp grounds in the Greer Recreation Area (59.0). Twelve miles further on you pass by McNary (71.0), located just off the highway, from where it is only 10 miles on into Pinetop.

Shortly beyond Pinetop camping is available at Lakeside (87.0). In the summer this campground is a popular stopping place and is often full on weekends. From Lakeside to Showlow traffic is sometimes heavy and the highway is shoulderless, so exercise care.

WHITE MOUNTAIN LOOP RIDE

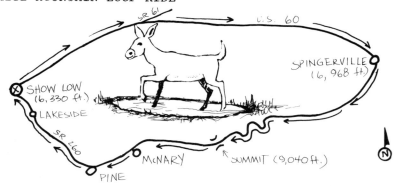

PRESCOTT - FLAGSTAFF

*SYNOPSIS: The journey from Prescott to Flagstaff is only for the well-conditioned cyclist. The trip involves about 7,000 of climbing, as it ascends both Mingus Mountain and the Oak Creek Canyon switchbacks. The route passes through the resurrected ghost town*

*of Jerome, perched precariously on the face of Mingus
Mountain, overlooking the vast Verde Valley and the
Sedona Red Rock Country.*

ROUND-TRIP: 93 miles. All day: 8-10 hours, or two
days if you prefer. Elevation gain-loss: 7,000 feet.
Season: late spring to early fall. Best day and time
to ride: any time, although there is less traffic in
Oak Creek Canyon on weekdays.

This demanding ride takes you from the open pasture
land around Prescott to the tall pines of Flagstaff
via one of the most exciting routes in Arizona.
Steep climbs, thrilling descents and spectacular
scenery make this a pedaling adventure for a cyclist
prepared for the arduous demands of the trip.
For those who prefer to make the trip in two days
there are good campgrounds in Oak Creek Canyon, midpoint of the ride. However, overnight camping means
carrying touring equipment, which makes the climbs
that much more difficult.
The roads are lightly traveled except in Oak Creek
Canyon, particularly on weekends when the canyon is
often as busy as a city street. Roadways are narrow
and shoulders are almost non-existent, so caution is
essential. Jerome in particular requires good bike
handling because the streets are cobblestoned. This
is definitely not a ride for beginners.
The route begins in mile-high Prescott (0.0) at
the town square. Follow U.S. 89 northward for five
miles and turn right onto 89A. The road now descends
into Prescott Valley, dropping below the 4,000-foot
level before rising again. Winds are usually constant
and often strong in this valley. The first hard climb
begins at the bottom of Mingus Mountain (17.0). Just
beyond the summit (22.) which is 7,743-feet high
your pass Potato Patch Campground (23.0). From here
to Jerome the descent is rapid, with many tight turns
and a few switchbacks. After rains, some of the turns
are sand-covered.
Jerome sits half-way down the eastern side of Mingus Mountain (31.0). Once world-famous for its rich

silver and copper mines, Jerome was abandoned and became a ghost town. In more recent decades it has become a haven for artists, craftsmen and retirees.
From its terraced streets you have a fantastic view
of the Verde Valley, and on clear days you can see
the San Francisco Peaks behind Flagstaff, your ulti-
mate destination.

After carefully negotiating Jerome, there is another thrilling descent to the eastern base of Mingus
Mountain. At the bottom you pass the turn-off (36.0)
to Clarkdale, also a former mining community. Turn
right and stay on 89A, which will take you through
part of Cottonwood (43.0) before you head north toward Sedona and Oak Creek Canyon on the other side
of the valley.

Between Cottonwood and Sedona the terrain gradually rises, and the road crosses numerous short hills
with occasional steep climbs. At the junction of 89A
and SR 179 (61.0) continue on 89A by turning left.
Sedona proper lies just over the hill (62.0).

Follow 89A through Sedona and on into Oak Creek
Canyon, being especially cautious if the traffic is
heavy. The tall pines, the cooling air and sparkling
Oak Creek make this portion especially pleasant (you
may want to stop at Slide Rock and take a refreshing
plunge in the popular mountain stream). There are
three campgrounds in the canyon. The largest one,
Cave Springs, is nearest the head of the canyon and
the switchbacks that take you up to the high plateau
country.

The switchback ascent (75.0) is very steep in some
places, but altogether is only three miles long. From
the top, it is 18 miles on into Flagstaff through a
canopy of beautiful pine and birch trees.

PRESCOTT-FLAGSTAFF RIDE MAP

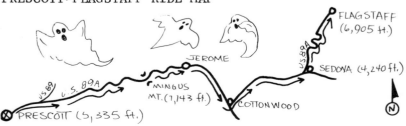

## WICKENBURG - PRESCOTT

*SYNOPSIS: This overnight trip is both challenging and spectacular, taking you up out of the picturesque desert country via the sheer escarpment of Yarnell Hill to high plateau country, and then on into the world's largest stand of Ponderosa pine, surrounding Prescott. On the way back you pass through Skull Valley, site of an infamous Indian massacre.*

ROUND-TRIP: 132 miles. Time required: two days. Elevation gain-loss: 3,200 feet. Season: mid-spring to early fall. Best day and time to ride: any time.

The trip begins in Wickenburg (0.0), the Dude Ranch Capital of the World, 50 miles northwest of Phoenix. Take U.S. 89/93 from the center of town northward. The first section of the ride takes you through lush desert flora, with spectacular views in all directions. At mile-6 U.S. 89 swings more to the northward. Stay on it. After you pass Congress Junction (16.0) there is a short downgrade then a gradual rise to the base of Yarnell Hill where the highway divides and the climb begins in earnest. It is seven miles to the top, and is steep in places, but the view you have on the way and from the top is one of the grandest in Arizona.

The town of Yarnell sits back only a few hundred yards from the edge of Yarnell Hill, amidst huge boulders and tall trees. Here you can stock up on natural artesian well water and other supplies.

From Yarnell you descend slightly into long Peeples Valley with its lush grazing lands. After Kirkland Junction (37.0) the road begins a gradual climb, then you hit a series of steep switchbacks that spiral you up into pine country. From the summit (48.), which is 6,000 feet high, it is a welcome 8-mile descent into Prescott.

Good camping is available in the Prescott National Forest just before you reach the main business section.

You may want to return via the same route but it

makes for a more interesting tour to swing around
through Skull Valley (see the Prescott-Skull Valley
Ride), rejoining U.S. 89 at Kirkland Junction.

WICKENBURG-PRESCOTT RIDE MAP

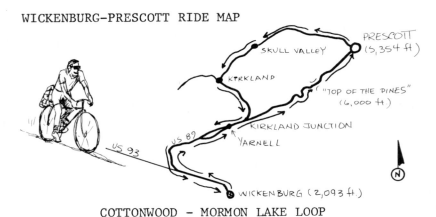

COTTONWOOD - MORMON LAKE LOOP

*SYNOPSIS: This long overnight loop trip is high-
lighted by the ascent of picturesque Oak Creek Canyon, a night beneath the towering pines surrounding
Mormon Lake, and a rapid descent of the spectacular
Mogollon Rim via a little traveled back road.*

ROUND-TRIP: 168 miles (77 the first day; 91 the second day). Time required: two days. Elevation loss-
gain: 3,500 feet. Season: late spring to early fall.
Best day and time to ride: anytime, but traffic can
be heavy in the Oak Creek Canyon area on weekends.

This bicycle camping trip has long been popular
with Arizona cyclists, especially on weekends. Starting point is Cottonwood (0.0), a small town just off
the Phoenix-Flagstaff highway in Verde Valley, about
100 miles north of Phoenix.
Follow U.S. 89A across Verde Valley into the Red
Rock Country to Sedona (20.0), continue on through
Sedona and up scenic Oak Creek Canyon. The canyon
road is narrow and crowded on weekend afternoons, so
start early enough that you are through it before
noon. The only really strenuous portion are the three
miles of switchbacks that take you out of the canyon

to the top of the Flagstaff plateau. An overlook at
the top provides a good view back down the canyon.
(It is 12 miles from Sedona to the base of the switchbacks.)

The next 16 miles is a gradual ascent toward Flagstaff that provides  you with provocative glimpses of
the San Francisco Peaks behind Flagstaff, as seen
through breaks in the dense pine and birch forest.

Just before reaching Flagstaff proper, turn right
onto Lake Mary Road (48.0). After another short ride
through more pines, the road crests a small hill and
begins to parallel Lake Mary. After passing this lake,
turn right onto Mormon Lake Road (69.0). A little further on you come to Rainy Springs Campgrounds, the
first of two in this area. The second one, Double
Springs (77.0) is preferable because large trailers
are prohibited. Elevation here is 7,200 feet, and
the area is dense with beautiful pines.

On the second day continue on around Mormon Lake.
At the Lake Mary Road "T", two miles from the camp
grounds, turn right toward Happy Jack and Clint's
Wells. In the next 30 miles only a Ranger Station at
Happy Jack and an occasional building marks the hand
of man in this dense forest. The terrain is flat or
rolling. At Clint's Wells (30.0) turn right onto SR
87 and proceed southward. Between Clint's Wells and
Camp Verde, 45 miles away, there are no facilities
for food or water.

Twelve miles from Clint's Wells, turn right onto
the Camp Verde Road (42.0). Shortly after this turn
you begin the long descent off the Mogollon Rim, one
of the longest and highest escarpments in the U.S.,
once again leaving the alpine high country for the
desert below. At Camp Verde in the middle of beautiful Verde Valley (75.0), the highway becomes SR 279.
Follow it west to the Flagstaff-Phoenix highway
(79.0) and continue on westward along the Verde River
to Cottonwood (91.0).

This trip takes you through some of the most fabulous semi-desert, canyon, forested highlands and
mountain country in the world, and deserves to be
done at a leisurely pace. See map on the next page.

## COTTONWOOD–MORMON LAKE RIDE MAP

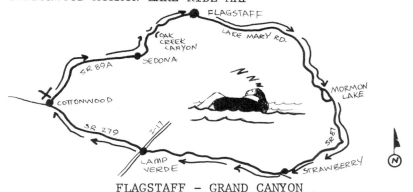

FLAGSTAFF – GRAND CANYON

*SYNOPSIS: This overnight tour takes you from Flag-staff, around the waist of the towering San Francisco Peaks, to the Grand Canyon, one of the world's most extraordinary natural wonders. The route includes several viewpoints along the rim of the canyon that give you a deep feeling of its majesty.*

ROUND-TRIP: 164 miles (72 miles each day). Time required: two days. Elevation loss-gain: 400 feet. Season: midspring to late fall. Best day and time: anytime.

The ride around the base of San Francisco Peaks, through forests of pine and birch is in itself worth the effort. Then you strike out across a high, windswept plateau, re-entering the pines just before you reach the canyon. When you do reach the rim's edge it comes as a surprise. The 8-mile paved road along the rim to Hermit's Rest is particularly suited to bicycle touring because only propane-powered National Park Service buses are permitted on the road.

This ride can easily be made in two days, but you might want to take more time and include a hike into the canyon.

From Flagstaff (0.0) head north on U.S. 180. The highway is two-lane and shoulderless, but the traffic is usually light once you are away from the city. Also, facilities are few and far between so take two water bottles and a couple of snacks along. Shortly after you pass the Snow Bowl Ski Area turn-off (7.0) the road drops down to a high plateau, which continues all the way to the canyon rim. It is mostly flat with only occasional gentle upgrades.

At mile-51 U.S. 180 meets SR 64, and the two merge. Turn right and continue on northward. A gradual rise begins here. Just before you reach the entrance to Grand Canyon National Park (74.0), where you have to pay a 50¢ vehicle fee, you are again among pines (small and stunted at first).

Where the highway crosses Rim Drive, turn left to go to the park headquarters for campground reservations and other facilities. The scenic 8-mile ride along the edge of the canyon begins here.

Those with the time and an adventurous spirit may choose to return via SR 64, which goes straight south toward Williams amd connects with old U.S. 66. Or you may take a much more scenic return route by heading east on U.S. 80/SR 64 which parallels the might Colorado River to Cameron, and there turn south on U.S. 89. The elevation at Grand Canyon Village on the South Rim is 6,876 feet. At Cameron it is 4,201 feet, and at Flagstaff 6,905 feet. So this alternate route is longer (26 miles) and requires more climbing.

FLAFSTAFF-GRAND CANYON RIDE MAP

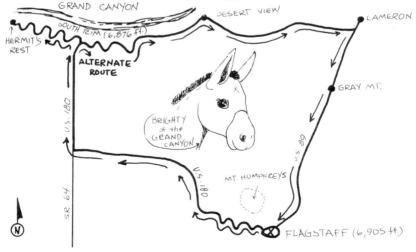

## FLAGSTAFF - STRAWBERRY

*SYNOPSIS: Another overnight trip, this ride takes you through dense pine forests, along silvery lakes and some of the most scenic spots in the state.*

ROUND-TRIP: 148 miles total. Time required: two days. Elevation gain-loss: 1,200 feet. Season: summer. Best day and time: any time.

Starting point for this ride is the intersection of SR 89A and Lake Mary Road, one mile south of Flagstaff proper (0.0.). The roads throughout the trip are fairly wide with adquate shoulders for bicycling, and for mile-after-mile the roadway is shaded from direct sunlight by high pine trees.

Proceed east on Lake Mary Road toward Mormon Lake. The section alongside Lake Mary (4.0) is especially scenic. At the Mormon Lake Lodge turn-off turn right if you want to visit the lodge. Otherwise proceed straight and continue on Lake Mary Road past Happy Jack Ranger Station (42.0). All of this area is dense with huge pine trees. There are a few gentle hills.

Clint's Wells is at the junction of Lake Mary Road and SR 87 (54.0). Food and water are available here. Turn right onto SR 87, go past the turn-off to Camp Verde (64.0), and begin the long descent off of the Mogollon Rim down to the town of Strawberry. There is good camping at the Pine Recreation Area near Strawberry (74.0). Return via the same route.

FLAGSTAFF-STRAWBERRY RIDE MAP

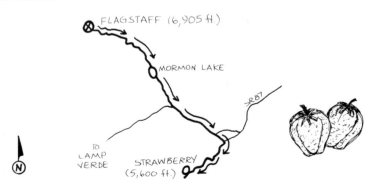

## NORTH RIM OF THE GRAND CANYON

*SYNOPSIS: This overnight trip into one of Arizona's more remote areas, the north side of the Grand Canyon, takes you away from the crowds and the traffic where the scenery has remained unchanged for millions of years.*

ROUND-TRIP: 120 miles (from Jacob's Lake, and including a 20-mile scenic ride along the canyon's edge). Time required: two days. Elevation gain-loss: 2,000 feet. Season: summer. Best day and time: any time.

    The starting point is the small community of Jacob's Lake 100 miles north of Flagstaff (0.0.). Go south on SR 67 over high plateau pasture land. The grade begins rising and you enter an every thickening pine forest. By the time you pass Kaibab Lodge (33.0) the climb has become uniformly steep--or at least it seems that way because of the altitude (nearly 8,000 feet).

    You enter the Grand Canyon National Park at mile 38 (50-cent fee), and continue on to the National Park Recreation Area (45.0), where food, lodging and camping are available. The scenic 20-mile ride to Point Imperial and Cape Royal begins here.

    You could take an extra day to adequately visit all the viewpoints, and possibly hike into the canyon. Keep in mind that the high altitude here (8,200 feet) means that winter lasts longer and comes earlier than it does at the South Rim of the Canyon. Roads within the canyon are narrow and shoulderless and there are frequent curves, but the traffic is usually very light.

    The return trip by the same route is a breeze.

NORTH RIM GRAND CANYON RIDE MAP

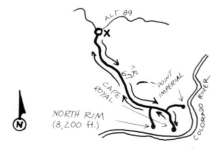

## SONOITA - BISBEE

*SYNOPSIS: This is an overnight trip suited for mid-winter as well as other seasons. The semi-loop is highlighted by a visit to Tombstone, "the town too tough to die," and Bisbee, a former mining center nestled in the Mule Mountains.*

ROUND-TRIP: 129 miles (63 miles the first day; 66 the second day). Time required: two days. Elevation gain-loss: 1,400 feet. Season: mid-winter to spring; also the fall. Best day and time to ride: any time.

The Sonoita-Bisbee Overnight Loop is a popular midwinter and early spring ride. It begins in the small cattle-rancher town of Sonoita 60 miles southeast of Tucson, in an area that reminded early Spanish settlers of Spain (which accounts for the town named Patagonia nearby). From Sonoita (0.0) head east on SR 82 through rich grasslands, gradually ascending a long hill before dropping to intersect SR 90 (19.0). Continue straight on SR 82. After a 16-mile stretch, memorable for a long descent and then a rapid climb out of a river bed (long since dry!), SR 82 meets U.S. 80 at the 35-mile mark. Turn right onto 80 and proceed up a long hill to Tombstone, once the most notorious town in the West where Wyatt Earp was the marshal and the famous shootout at OK Corral took place.

Leave Tombstone on U.S. 80 going south. The highway descends into a long valley before swinging east toward the Mule Mountains. The 8-mile climb up to Mule Pass begins where 80 intersects SR 90.

Bisbee (63.0) is just on the other side of the summit of the pass, but there are two ways of getting there: one through a tunnel and the other one over the top. Going through the tunnel and exiting one mile further along for downtown Bisbee is the easiest but going over the top is the most interesting.

To take the scenic route turn onto the unsigned Old Mule Pass Road on the left, just before the tunnel. Old Mule Pass Overlook is a mile's climb up this road. The overlook provides a panoramic view of Bisbee as well as a long view toward Mexico.

Continue on this unsigned road and enter Bisbee via the old highway. Shortly after the Iron Man Statue the old highway joins the new highway, but continue on down Tombstone Canyon, as the main road is now called, to the business district.

To return, after an overnight stop in Bisbee, go south out of Bisbee on U.S. 80. A short way beyond spectacular Lavender Open Pit Mine, turn right onto SR 92 (2.0). From here its three miles to the Naco turn-off (Naco is in Mexico, four miles away and is an interesting side-trip).

Stay on SR 92 going west past the Hereford turn-off (17.0). As the highway nears the Hauchuca Mountains it veers north. Continue through tiny Nicksville (23.0). Shortly thereafter 92 meets SR 90, and ends. (31.0). Go north on 90 to Sierra Vista (39.0), on the waist of the spectacular Huachuca Mountains, and with a magnificient view of the surrounding countryside and other nearby mountains.

The next community is Huachuca City (43.0), just beyond which 90 crosses SR 82. Turn left and take 82 back to Sonoita.

SONOITA-BISBEE RIDE MAP

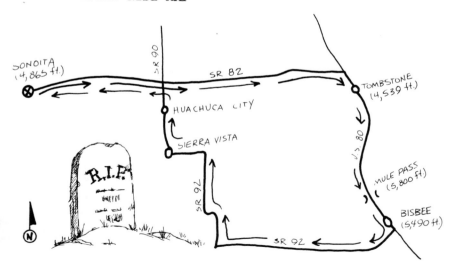

## AJO - ORGAN PIPE OVERNIGHT

*SYNOPSIS: A visit to the famous Organ Pipe National Monument, a huge forest of organ pipe cacti as well as other cacti found nowhere else in the U.S., is the principal reason for this unusual trip. If you are really adventurous, Mexico is only a short distance way from the monument entrance.*

ROUND-TRIP: 68 miles. Time recommended: two days. Elevation gain-loss: minimal. Season: early spring is best; fall is next. Best day and time: any time.

The trip begins in Ajo, the well-known copper mining town (0.0). Head south on SR 85 toward Why (10.0). The terrain is mostly flat. A little beyond Why you arrived at the boundary of Organ Pipe National Monument (14.0), from which point the scenery becomes almost incredibly beautiful. From there it is 20 miles to Monument Visitor's Center and campgrounds.

The journey can easily be made in a few hours but it is worth taking two days to explore the two loop rides within the monument: a 21-mile loop into the Ajo Mountains, and the Puerto Blanco 30-mile loop to Quitobaquito, a marshy swamp visited by migratory birds. The Mexican border is five miles from the campgrounds.

AJO-ORGAN PIPE MONUMENT RIDE MAP

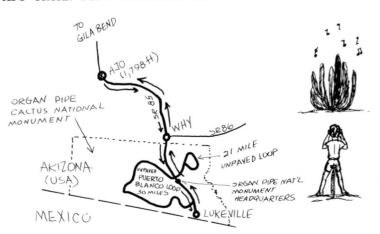

## CENTRAL ARIZONA LOOP

*SYNOPSIS: This is a long loop ride for the ambitious, well-prepared and well-conditioned bicycle tourist. The tour takes one out of the central Arizona desert to Flagstaff via Wickenburg, Prescott, Jerome and Sedona. The return route is via Mormon Lake, Strawberry, Payson and Sunflower--giving the bicyclist a generous sampling of all the different types of natural scenic beauty in Arizona.*

ROUND-TRIP: 370 miles. Time required: four to seven days. Elevation gain-loss: 10,000 feet. Season: late spring to early fall.

This challenging tour can be divided into two sections. The first involves the ascent from Phoenix (el. 1,100 feet) to Flagstaff (6,900 feet). The distance on this leg is 200 miles, and there are several long, steep climbs: Yarnell Hill, the "Top of the Pines" summit just before Prescott, Mingus Mountain on the way to Jerome/Sedona, and the switchbacks out of Oak Creek Canyon. The return leg from Flagstaff to Phoenix is mostly downhill, and is shorter--170 miles.

Traffic from Phoenix to Wickenburg via U.S. 60/70 can be fairly heavy, but the highway is wide, with good shoulders for the entire distance. For details about the route from Wickenburg, see the Wickenburg-Prescott, Prescott-Flagstaff and Flagstaff-Strawberry sections. From Strawberry to Payson, continue south on SR 87. There is a long gradual climb up to Payson that starts just after you pass through Pine.

The Payson to Phoenix section begins with a rapid descent out of Payson. After Rye the terrain is rolling until you come to a long climb followed by a descent into Sunflower. After Sunflower there is a series of hills, one of them quite long, bringing you back to the Fountain Hills/Scottsdale area.

As far as scenic beauty, variety of terrain and interesting stopovers, this is one of the best possible rides in Arizona.

See map on next page.

CENTRAL ARIZONA LOOP RIDE MAP

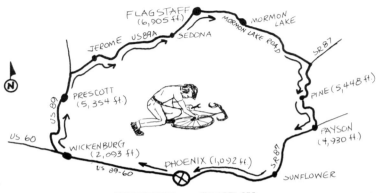

SUPERIOR – SHOWLOW

*SYNOPSIS: This demanding but richly rewarding tour, from the foothills east of the Valley of the Sun into the spectacular White Mountains via the Salt River Canyon, is another choice Arizona bicycle tour. Among its highlights are the Salt River Canyon and the White Mountain Apache Indian Reservation.*

ROUND-TRIP: 235 miles. Time required: four or five days. Elevation gain-loss: over 3,000 feet. Season: early spring to early fall. Any day.

This ride begins and ends in Superior, a mining town 50 miles east of Phoenix. Depart Superior (0.0) on U.S. 60 and ascend through Queen Creek Tunnel to the "Top of the World" summit. A rapid descent past Blue Bird Copper Mine brings you to Miami (26.0). From here continue on U.S. 60 to Globe (34.0).

Just beyond Globe, where U.S. 60 and 70 intersect, stay on U.S. 60 by turning left (also SR 77) and head north. Shortly after Jones Water (50.) the road begins climbing toward an unsigned summit which marks the entrance into Salt River Canyon. From the summit there are five miles of switchbacks down to the bridge over Salt River (62.0). Beneath the bridge is a campgrounds where the first day normally ends. There is a small store near the bridge.

Day two begins with an ascent to the Salt River Canyon's north rim; a 5-mile ride that is quite steep in places. The next facilities are at Carrizo, 29 miles away, so take plenty of water. After Carrizo (91.0) the terrain becomes rolling pasture land, and then pine forests as you approach the Showlow area.

At the intersection of U.S. 60 and SR 260 (122.0), turn right onto 260 and proceed east toward Lakeside and Pinetop. A campground at Lakeside marks the end of day two, and the half-way point in the tour.

From Lakeside (0.0) continue on 260 through Pinetop (3.0) to SR 73 (6.0). Turn right onto 73 and proceed south toward Whiteriver, headquarters of the White Mountain Apache tribe. The gradual descent takes you out of the pine trees of the White Mountains back into the pastureland that is common to the 5,000-ft. level in Arizona.

Continue on SR 73 to the junction with U.S. 60 at the 50-mile mark. Turn left onto U.S. 60 and head back toward the Salt River Canyon. The third night is usually spent at the Salt River Canyon campgrounds; returning to Superior the following day.

This trip can be made less strenuous by taking an extra day in Lakeside to rest and look around.

SUPERIOR-SHOWLOW RIDE MAP

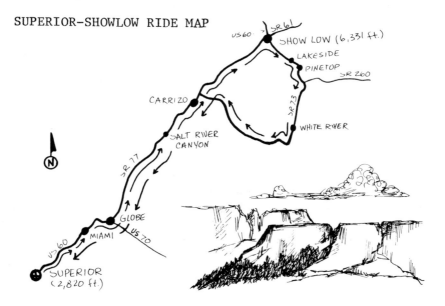

## NAVAJO - HOPI LOOP

*SYNOPSIS: This long ride, through the heart of Hopi Land and the Navajo Nation is a once-in-a-lifetime experience. The route takes you to the high mesa villages of the Hopi (one of them being the oldest continuously inhabited community in the country), and Canyon De Chelly, one of the most spectacular and poignant settings on earth. The distances are vast but coming across a Navajo hogan or sheepherder in the vastness is an extraordinary experience that makes it worthwhile.*

ROUND-TRIP: 320 miles. Time required: five to seven days. Elevation gain-loss: 3,000 feet. Season: summer.

   This is a long, sometimes difficult, loop-tour for the experienced cyclist who is prepared for the unexpected and wants to travel off the beaten path. The route traverses the canyon and mesa lands of northern Arizona. Vistas are immense and the scenery is grander than imaginable.
   The uniqueness of the Hopi villages make them fascinating places to visit. Background reading on the Hopi way of life, their beliefs and religion, is essential for an understanding of a way of life that has changed little over the centuries. Cameras are forbidden in some of the villages and at most of the ceremonies. You must have a guide to visit some of the more sacred places. Obey all signs and keep out of areas forbidden to non-Hopi's.
   Trading posts on the two reservations are few and far between and they operate at irregular hours, but they are the only source of food and sometimes water as well for many miles around. Carry adequate supplies and have an itinerary that is flexible enough to deal with the unexpected.
   Roads along the route are usually narrow and shoulderless. In places they are in a poor state of repair. Where they cross washes, they are often in especially bad shape.  Motor traffic is light but cars often travel at high speeds along these narrow roads.

Daily mileage estimates are not presented for this tour. It is too long and offers too many interesting variations to suggest firm travel plans. Each group should be flexible enough to adapt to daily weather conditions and spur-of-the-moment decisions. Camping is available at numerous locations along the route (for campsites, see *Outdoor Recreation in Arizona* by Bob Golden, available from Phoenix Books).

Starting point is Tuba City, 120 miles northeast of Flagstaff. Head east on SR 264, which will take you into the heart of Hopi Land. After visiting the Hopi villages, continue on 264 to Keams Canyon, which boasts an especially beautiful campgrounds. At the intersection of 264 and SR 63, turn left onto 63 and go northward toward Chinle and Canyon de Chelly. Guided tours into the canyon are available.

From Canyon De Chelly continue on north past Many Farms, Round Rock and Rock Point to Mexican Water where SR 63 meets U.S. 160. Turn west and head back southwest through Dennehotso, Kayenta, Tsegi, Cow Springs and Tonalea to Tuba City. This portion takes you by Monument Valley, which is one of the most stunningly beautiful places on earth, and Navajo National Monument.

Also highly recommended reading: *Visitor's Guide to Arizona's Indian Reservations* by Boye De Mente, available from Phoenix Books.

NAVAJO-HOPI RIDE MAP

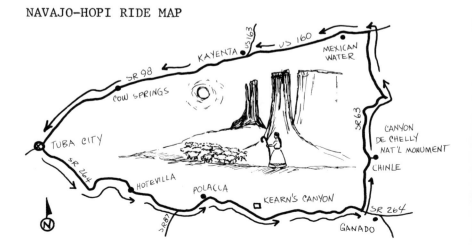

## ACROSS ARIZONA – WEST TO EAST

*SYNOPSIS: For many Arizona bicyclists the supreme experience is to cross the entire state by bicycle, and there is a well-traveled route designed for just that. The route is part of the Southwest Bicycle Trail, which links up with the Bikecentennial Cross-Country Route in Kansas. The west-east ride avoids the larger cities and gives one an extraordinary view of the nation's fourth largest state.*

ONE-WAY: 540 miles. Time required: one week to 10 days. Elevation gain-loss: around 10,000 feet. Season: late spring to early fall.

The Arizona section of the Southwest Bicycle Trail begins in Yuma and leaves the state just outside of Window Rock on the Navajo Indian Reservation. The route is mainly along lightly traveled roads, so the major concern is the heat of the desert and unexpected weather conditions.

On the first desert portions of the trip, you should start early each morning, just as soon as the center strip of the highway is discernable. Travel at a moderate but steady pace throughout the morning hours. During the hottest hours, rest and sleep. If there is no natural shade, a tent or poncho can be erected. Additional mileage can be made in the evening hours.

Carry a lot of water and drink freely. Replenish the supply at every opportunity. Study your copy of the Arizona Highway Map carefully in advance to plan each day's ride to avoid running out of water, and carry some extra in case of an emergency.

Protect your head with a helmet or hat. Wear a covering over the back of your neck. Keep the covering damp to provide additional cooling. Wear a long-sleeved white shirt. Wear sunscreen on your face and other areas of the skin exposed to the sun.

From Yuma (in the extreme southwest corner of the state) head north on U.S. 95. At Quartzsite turn right onto U.S. 60 and proceed east to Aguila. Take SR 71

until it links up with U.S. 89 at Congress. Take 89
through Prescott to where it meets 89A. Follow 89A
through Jerome and Sedona to Flagstaff.

From Flagstaff continue on U.S. 89 to the U.S. 60
junction. Take U.S. 60 to where it intersects with
SR 264 at Tuba City. Proceed east on 264 through the
Hopi Indian Reservation and the Navajo Nation to Window Rock, Navajo tribal headquarters. Your journey
ends just two miles from Window Rock at the Arizona-
New Mexico border.

(The Southwest Bicycle Trail was mapped in 1978 by
cyclists from the Southwest who wanted a more direct
route to join up with the Trans American Bicycle
Trail which begins in Astoria, Oregon and goes to York-
town, Virginia. The Trans American trail was deliber-
ately planned to avoid the hot deserts of the South-
west--but in doing so did not serve the interests of
bicyclists in this area. More information is available
from: Southwest Bicycle Trail, 816 Van Buren, Amarillo,
Texas 79101; also, Bikecentennial, P.O. Box 8308, Mis-
soula, Montana 59807.)

ACROSS ARIZONA RIDE MAP

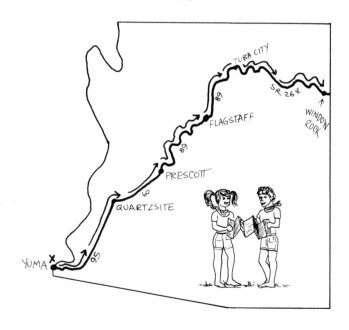

# ARIZONA BICYCLING ORGANIZATIONS

Like most other activity, bicycling is a lot more fun when done with someone else. It is especially helpful for novice riders to participate in outings with more experienced bicyclists. The following Arizona bicycling organizations welcome new members.

AYH PHOENIX--The American Youth Hostels, Phoenix, conducts breakfast rides from various locations on Saturday and Sunday mornings. It also occasionally conducts longer rides. The AYH publishes the monthly Arizona Hosteler, which lists scheduled rides. For more information, contact the AYH, 1049 N. 38th Pl., Phoenix, Az 85032.

CABA (Central Arizona Bicycling Association)--Arizona's largest bicycle club, CABA regularly conducts seminars on better biking practices, and promotes organized short and long tours. CABA also publishes the monthly Arizona Bicycling Update. Contact: CABA, 1032 E. Henry St., Tempe, Az 85281.

COSMIC CYCLING CLUB--A Flagstaff-based club which promotes races and schedules training rides on a regular basis. Contact: 115 S. San Francisco St., Flagstaff, Az 86001.

CUREGHEM APOLLINARS SPORTIF--Tempe-based club founded to promote bicycle racing. Also conducts training rides. Contact: 920 S. Terrace #110, Tempe, Az 85281.

LAS TOURISTAS--A Tucson club which promotes bicycle touring; conducts local rides weekly and occasionally long tours. Publishes a monthly ride schedule. Contact: 3450 N. Stone Ave., #171, Tucson, Az 85705.

PHOENIX CONSUMER'S CYCLING CLUB--Arizona's oldest bicyling club, promotes races and conducts training rides on a regular schedule. Contact: 5040 E. Sheridan, Phoenix, Az 85008.

PIMA VELO CLUB--A Tucson bicycle racing club. Contact: P.O. Box 43326, Tucson, Az 85721.

TUCSON WHEELMEN--A Tucson-based racing and touring club that conducts weekly training rides; occasional tours. Contact: 1016 Chauncey, Tucson, Az 85719.

# Other Phoenix Books Publications of Special Interest

**VISITOR'S GUIDE TO ARIZONA'S INDIAN RESERVATIONS**
By Boye De Mente. ISBN: 0-914778-14-5. Trade
paperback. $3.95

The sightseeing attractions, spectator events,
ceremonial dances and public recreational facilities on each Reservation; plus maps.

**ARIZONA TOURIST & MILEAGE MAP**
All of Arizona's natural wonders, monuments,
wilderness areas, Indian Reservations and man-
made attractions illustrated and described; plus
miles between all points on every highway in the
state. $1.50

**ILLUSTRATED SIGHTSEEING MAP OF ARIZONA**
Shows the state's 63 most famous attractions in
full color, with descriptions and miles from
Phoenix/Scottsdale/Tucson. $1.50. Large poster
version available, $5

**GUIDE TO OUTDOOR RECREATION IN ARIZONA**
By Bob Golden. ISBN: 0-914778-09-9. Trade paperback. $3.00

Everything you might want to know about having
fun in Arizona's great outdoors, from sightseeing
and fishing to spectator sports and ghost towns.

**INSIDER'S GUIDE TO PHOENIX, SCOTTSDALE, TEMPE, MESA
& TUCSON**, by Boye De Mente. ISBN: 0-914778-05-6.
$3.00

Designed especially for visitors and newcomers,
from househunting, getting settled, licenses,
schools and eating out to special places to take
children.

**RETIRING IN ARIZONA--Senior Citizen's Shangri La**
By Boye De Mente. ISBN: 0-914778-07-2. $6.95

Packed with information vital to anyone interested
in retiring in wonderful Arizona.

PAT NEVE'S BODYBUILDING DIET BOOK, by Vicki Neve
ISBN: 0-914778-33-1. Illustrated. $6.00

The winner of over 100 bodybuilding titles and
one of the world's greatest bodybuilding champ-
ions, Pat Neve operates a gym in Phoenix. This
is the diet that helped make him the champion
he is. The 2nd edition includes a weight-gain
diet for young bodybuilders and athletes, a
weight-loss diet for those who are overweight,
and a special diet for women bodybuilders.

HOW TO AVOID & TREAT TENNIS ELBOW & OTHER COURT
INJURIES, by John Anthony & Michael Nacinovich.
ISBN: 0-914778-28-5. Trade paperback. $4.95

This unique and remarkable book represents a
break-thru in both the prevention and treatment
of the painful affliction known as tennis elbow.
The authors are the two leading tennis/racquet-
ball injury therapists in the country.

SIMPLIFIED GOLF: There's No Trick to It!
By Peter Longo. ISBN: 0-914778-34-X. Quality
paperback. The best golf book ever written. $7

HOW TO RIDE A BICYCLE SAFELY, EFFICIENTLY & PAIN-
LESSLY, by Anita Notdurft-Hopkins. ISBN: 0-
914778-27-7. Trade paperback. $2.95

Noted bicyclist/author Anita Notdurft-Hopkins
identifies and explains the proper techniques
for bicycle riding, as well as the psychology
of safe bicycling. Includes special sections
for parents who buy bikes for their children.

HOW TO GET ON THE BARTER BANDWAGON, by Mark Fournier.
ISBN: 0-914778-32-3. Quality trade paperback.
Illustrated. $6.00

Barter is back and is bigger and better than ever!
Learn how you can get almost anything you want
by trading for it! Find out how you can live
better with less cash!

HOW TO SURVIVE STRESS (In This Mad Mad World!)
By Dr. William West. ISBN: 0-914778-35-8.
Quality trade paperback. $6.00

The human body's violent reaction to stress--
a holdover from man's primitive past when we
were literally constructed to fight or flee in
the face of any obstacle, danger or fear--is
incompatible with modernday society, and is
therefore an insidious disease that threatens
us all. Internationally known educator/author/
lecturer Dr. Bill West tells how to recognize,
understand and measure stress, how to avoid
most of it, and how to live with what we cannot
avoid. An invaluable handbook for daily living.

EROTIC MEXICO: A Traveler's Unofficial Guide
By Richard Crownover. Papaerback. $2.00
ISBN: 0-914778-11-0.

All about Mexico's notorious masculinity cult,
playboy and playgirl activity on the local
scene; how foreign lovers make out, and more.

I LIKE YOU, GRINGO--BUT!, by Mario ("Mike") De La
Fuente. ISBN: 0-914778-08-0. Trade paperback.
$2.50

A warm, humorous, sensual, provocative story
of the life and times of Mike De La Fuente, a
pioneer in breaking the ethnic barrier in pro
American baseball, Mexico's most colorful bull-
fight impresario, indefatigable ladies' man
and reknowed trouble-shooter along the U.S.-
Mexican border for 40 years.

EROS' REVENGE: THE 'BRAVE NEW WORLD' OF AMERICAN
SEX, by Boye De Mente. ISBN: 0-914778-21-8.
Quality trade paperback. $6.95

A fascinating view of the misunderstanding, mis-
use and abuse of human sexuality; the resulting
frustrations, perversions and violence that
plague the U.S....and where the Sexual Revolution
is really going (including the emergence of a
matriarchal society and neighborhood sex centers
for people who can't get it anywhere else!).

SENSUAL YOGA--For Men & Women. ISBN: 0-914778-13-7
By Richard Crownover. Paperback. $1.50

Identifies, illustrates and explains the yoga
exercises that play a major role in slowing
the aging process, enhancing sexual vigor and
increasing longevity.

KICKING THE SMOKING HABIT, by Boye De Mente. ISBN:
0-914778-10-2. Paperback. $2.00

Clears up the myths and mysteries surrounding
the smoking habit, how it effects people dif-
ferently, and what it takes to break the habit.
A good gift for someone you care about.

FACE-READING FOR FUN & PROFIT, by Boye De Mente.
ISBN: 0-914778-18-8. Trade paperback. $2.95

Face-reading is as old as man, and is a univer-
sal art that all of us practice every day with
varying degrees of skill. This fascinating/fun
book goes behind those big blue eyes or little
beady eyes, those long bushy eyebrows, that
high, wide forehead or whatever and tells what
they mean in relation to character, health,
personality, sexual appetite, popularity and
life-expectancy.

MAGIC FACE-READING WHEEL
Allows anyone to become an expert at reading
faces in an instant. Makes anyone the life of
the party. Ideal gift for old and young alike.
Twelve inches in diameter. $3.95

ORDERING INFORMATION

If these publications are not available at your
book store, order from Phoenix Books/Publishers,
P.O. Box 32008, Phoenix, Arizona 85064. Add 75¢
to the price of the first book (single book order),
plus 25¢ for each additional title (on the same
order) for packaging and shipping.

| 10-5 Sun | Mummy Mountain. 15 mi. 1:15, Light Traffic. |
|----------|----------------------------------------------|
| 10-11 Sat | Thunderbird Park — leg (23 mi), 3:00. Light Traffic. Bad headwind on return leg. |
| 10-18 Sat | Pinnacle Peak loop — climb (24 mi.) 2:40. moderate/heavy traffic (noon) |